Milton Osborne

# Region of Revolt

# Focus on Southeast Asia

Penguin Books

Penguin Books Ltd, Harmondsworth,
Middlesex, England
Penguin Books Australia Ltd, Ringwood,
Victoria, Australia

First published by Pergamon Press, Australia, 1970
Published in Pelican Books 1971
Copyright © Milton Osborne, 1970

Printed in Australia for Penguin Books
Australia Ltd at Halstead Press, Sydney
Set in Linotype Baskerville

# Contents

Introduction 9
1 Images of Revolt 11
2 Traditional Patterns of Revolt 18
3 Tradition in a Colonial Context 34
4 Seed Time of Revolt: The Years Before
   the Second World War 52
5 The Second World War 74
6 Malaya and the Philippines:
   Two Revolts that Failed 88
7 The Revolt that Half Succeeded 111
8 The Myth-Ridden War 130
9 Toppling the God-King 159
10 Theorists and Theories 169
11 Region of Revolt 184
Bibliography 195
Index 199

'Wars are never fought for one reason,' he said. 'They are fought for dozens of reasons, in a muddle. It is the same with revolts.'

Merlyn, in
*The Queen of Air and Darkness*
by T. H. White

# Introduction

Few subjects have received such widespread attention in the sixties as the phenomenon of revolt and revolutionary change in Southeast Asia. The agonizing experience of the war in Viet-Nam has focused attention on events in that country and brought some examination of other instances of revolt in Southeast Asia since the Second World War. But despite the interest which has been aroused in the problem of revolt, the bulk of the material which has appeared on the subject has been written by those with a professional interest in the subject or the area, and for an audience of professionals. At the wider level, the discussion which has taken place has frequently been conducted at a remarkably low level both of competence and understanding.

This short book, as its sub-title indicates, represents reflections on the problem of revolt in Southeast Asia. The book expresses personal views and it has a case to argue, or possibly more correctly several cases. Above all, it is an attempt to place contemporary instances of revolt in some historical perspective as an alternative to the all too common approach to the problem which ignores the background to current developments.

I am grateful that Dr Andrew Fabinyi should have suggested to me that academics ought to discipline themselves to write for a wider audience than the world of scholarship. For a writer used to buttressing his points with footnotes it is a challenge to try and make points stand on their own. Dr Fabinyi's encouragement was most important throughout the preparation of the manuscript. I have a special debt of gratitude to those students at Monash University who stimulated and refined my thoughts on the

Introduction

subject of revolt in Southeast Asia in the course of a seminar on the subject during 1968 and 1969.

Having expressed my thanks, however, I must emphasize that I alone bear responsibility for the statements made and the views expressed in this book.

*Milton Osborne*
*Monash University, 1970*

Introduction to Pelican Edition

In revising the text for the Pelican edition of *Region of Revolt* I have tried to take account of various criticisms and suggestions offered by readers and reviewers. This has resulted in some minor shifts of emphasis but no major change in the basic argument: that contemporary instability in Southeast Asia stems from deep-seated historical causes as much as from immediate political considerations.

Amongst those who have made helpful suggestions, I am particularly grateful for the detailed commentary and advice on my text provided by Professor John Legge of Monash University.

More detailed treatment is given in this edition to the events in Cambodia associated with the overthrow of Prince Sihanouk in 1970. Much of the material incorporated in this new chapter originally appeared in *Current Affairs Bulletin*, Volume 47, No. 1, of 30 November 1970.

Once again, the responsibility for the contents of this book is mine alone.

*Milton Osborne*
*1971*

# Chapter 1

# Images of Revolt

The mark of revolt has scarred the history of Southeast Asia. On occasion revolts have become revolutions and so transformed a country or even a region. More often revolts have failed to achieve, and have even hampered, transformation. Yet some of the failures have been the bases for future successes as the unsuccessful revolt is built upon to provide a rallying point for action or a national myth which sustains the conviction of national identity. The ill-fated revolt of the Vietnamese Trung sisters in the first century AD did nothing at that time to rid Viet-Nam of its Chinese overlords. In succeeding centuries the sisters, both their characters and their achievements transmuted by legend, have become national symbols of Vietnamese resistance to China. As heroines, the Trung sisters in contemporary Viet-Nam have been at the heart of propaganda, both north and south of the seventeenth parallel, which has aimed at incorporating Vietnamese women in the affairs of the state.

The part legendary feats of the Trung sisters are now enshrined in images of brave but beautiful women leading their troops against the Chinese with elephants as their mounts. Choosing death rather than national dishonour, their heroism is remembered rather than the carnage which attended their failure. In more recent historical times, and above all in contemporary Southeast Asia, the human cost of revolt becomes clearer and the justification for revolt or for its suppression becomes less certain.

The modern images of revolt are less easily tinted by romantic hues. Where was the romance in the one major anti-colonial revolt of the Cambodians against French rule in the nineteenth century? The Cambodian Rising of 1885 and 1886 was a notable event in Cambodian history, if not so clearly nationalist in character as Cambodian government publications are now beginning to argue. In its two-year duration it caused some ten thousand deaths, mostly Cambodian; the destruction of some of the richest rice-growing areas of the country; and the emigration of perhaps forty thousand people out of Cambodia to escape from danger.

Few, indeed, of the anti-colonial revolts in Southeast Asia are redeemed by romance. Heroism and futility are present in quantity, as are cruelty and a blind ignorance of fact – on the part of both those who revolted and those who resisted revolt. The decision of Indonesian Communists to rise against the Dutch in 1926 and 1927 was a glaring example of a revolt for which the time was not ripe nor the most elementary planning prepared. No amount of special pleading has enabled the Communist apologists for this revolt to overcome the reality that activists revolted in conditions which were supremely unsuitable for success.

The record of revolt and suppression in Viet-Nam is possibly unequalled, for colonial times, anywhere else in Southeast Asia. In this pattern of Vietnamese revolt there was boundless courage, but little romance. For the nineteenth century one must conjure up the image of repeated risings against French power, bloodily repressed, more often than not by Vietnamese fighting on the French side. Men such as the southern Vietnamese Tran Ba Loc, a Catholic and an unhesitating supporter of the French position, were loosed upon their ill-armed compatriots to suppress and punish with a vigour which led even Loc's admiring French biographer, George Dürrwell, to have reservations about his actions.

In the twentieth century there are the images of poorly armed peasants, spurred on by Communist cadres to resist overwhelming French power in the desperately poor province of Nghe-An. This extraordinarily interesting example of revolt in which a modern party machine successfully enlisted the support of far from modern peasants has still to be investigated in depth. What is clear is the force with which the revolt was put down and the train of guillotining and exile which succeeded.

What had been desperate defiance in Nghe-An changed to carefully co-ordinated war when the Viet-Minh led a massive anti-colonial movement in the late 1940s and early 1950s. The costs of this revolt were staggering for both sides. Whether heroism redeems the symbolic end of the war – the capture of Dien-Bien-Phu – must be a personal judgement. French strategy was marked by an almost incredible degree of foolishness. Vietnamese strategy spent lives with abandon. The most telling picture of this battle is not to be found in the accounts of French *paras* dropping into certain defeat or in the dogged brilliance of Vo Nguyen Giap's forces setting their artillery where it was not expected. The image emerges in the immediate post-battle period when the victorious Vietnamese led their shattered prisoners past wounded Viet-Minh to the start of a death march which obliterated the moments of respect for battlefield courage which each side could hold during the course of the siege.

It is only in retrospect that revolts can be viewed with the detachment which permits any truly balanced understanding of the issues involved. One must react to the immediate facts which confront an observer if one has any sense of humanity. I can never entirely remove from my thoughts on Viet-Nam the sight of a woman without legs being wheeled to the delivery room in a Mekong Delta hospital. Nobody knew which side had laid the mine that had blown off her legs and yet had left her with an unborn child. But if the stark tragedy of such images affects the capacity which a student has to analyse events with a clarity unimpaired by personal feelings, one key issue is thrown into sharp relief. One cannot write of revolt without writing of individuals, their personalities and their beliefs. One cannot explain the outbreaks of revolt which have beset post-Second World War Southeast Asia solely in terms of skilful Communist organization. One cannot dismiss the weight of history when one writes of revolt, since even the simplest man who rises against authority – whether that authority is legitimate or not – is a child of history and of his country, or his region, or his village's historical experience.

Too often the explanation of revolt in Southeast Asia has been in simple terms. Dichotomies have been posed which have no relation to the events of the individuals involved. Debating whether Ho Chi Minh was a Communist or a nationalist has been a futile exercise for the West, if it really wished to understand the problems of Viet-Nam. The question of whether a man is a Communist or a nationalist is relevant in our society. It may be relevant in other countries of Southeast Asia. But for Viet-Nam in general, and for Ho in particular, the question becomes meaningless – a mis-statement of the problem. American officials in Saigon could still pose the question in 1966 while a South Vietnamese newspaper editor, his costs subsidized by the United States Government, could say of the National Liberation Front to his Australian visitor, 'Ils sont, aussi, nationalistes.'

It is not merely truth which is the first casualty of war and conflict. Falling beside truth are such other fundamentals as a careful regard for past events and an understanding of the complexities of issues. The past and its complexities must be understood if one is to grasp a central fact about Southeast Asia. This is a region of revolt. Its history and its present are troubled not only because of the ambitions of rebels or because of the expansionist aims of Communist governments. These influences can be important. But of great importance too are the indigenous factors of instability. The rivalries of race and ethnic division are perhaps most obvious. The colonial experience sustained by all but one of the countries of Southeast Asia left its own legacy of difficulties. It created firm boundaries where previously there had been none, and in doing so laid the basis for future conflict. Political decisions taken by colonial governments have led to continuing conflict as well as to successful revolutions.

Yet while the past illuminates the present there is a sad lack of information on many of the revolts of the past. The preoccupation of court chronicles with kings and events in the capitals has provided too little information about challenges to authority, unless authority was successfully attacked. For early Southeast Asian history our knowledge can sometimes be so fragmentary that we must deduce that there was a slave revolt in twelfth century Cambodia from a brief inscription and a scene recorded on a carved bas-relief.

The reluctance of court historians to tell of challenges to their masters was matched in modern colonial times by the reticence of Western administrators in Southeast Asia to publicize the revolts of those whom they administered. On some occasions the records pass quickly over the fact of revolt. At other times the records are detailed in their account of the anti-colonial revolts, but the information did not pass out of the privileged circles of government to become public knowledge.

Since the Second World War there have been major anti-colonial revolts in Indonesia, Malaya and Viet-Nam and an attempted Communist rising of very considerable proportions in the Philippines. These revolts have been the focus of attention, so that one easily forgets the almost continuous regional unrest in Burma or the major regional rebellions of 1958 in Indonesia. The changing demands of the news media regulate our information and our attention span is short. We seem to be able easily to forget an event or even an area if Western interests are not directly involved. The war in Viet-Nam has become an international obsession, but few take pause over the half million or more Indonesians who were killed after the failure of an unsuccessful revolt in Djakarta. An increasing tendency towards disunity in Cambodia, which was ignored by the West until the dramatic deposition of Prince Sihanouk early in 1970, showed the extent to which even this supposed haven of stability was troubled by fissiparous factors.

The entire Western vision of Southeast Asia still suffers from a distorted image of colonial times. The West has been disturbed by the increasing evidence in the years after the Second World War of Southeast Asia's lack of stability and predisposition to unrest just because of the survival of a distorted image. The now widely held view that colonialism is an undesirable phenomenon has not prevented men from thinking that colonialism was somehow synonymous with peace. As with every widely held though incorrect view there is a sufficient element of truth in this conviction for it to resist the now massive debunking which is being provided by historians and political scientists. For while colonial governments faced many more challenges to their authority than is usually recognized, these same governments did achieve success in freezing many of the traditional rivalries which were so much a feature of pre-colonial society. The French in Cambodia were at pains to discount the seriousness of the 1885–6 rising, but they did achieve a certain unity for Cambodia, a unity which the country had not known for centuries. The British in Burma faced various challenges to their authority of quite serious proportions, yet their presence was able to hold in abeyance the ethnic rivalry of Burmans and Shans.

The peace of colonialism was temporary and fragile. It disguised the dangers of future unrest. Only when this image is firmly established is it possible to comprehend the unsettled present and to face the prospect of a difficult future. New ideologies play their part in Southeast Asian revolts, but the links with the concerns of the past cannot be denied. It is as dangerously simple to dismiss the continuity in the appeal to revolt given out by the Viet-Cong as it would be to see these men as no more, no less, than 'agrarian reformers'.

Loosely speaking of 'modern' Southeast Asia we transfer to that region our own imagined image of modernity.

With rare exceptions Southeast Asia is not modern. Countries are states rather than nations,* seldom providing the opportunities for citizenship to all within their boundaries. The battle to control Viet-Nam has solid links with regional feeling in the past and with the Vietnamese search for an alternative world view to replace Confucianism, which failed so patently to provide an answer to the colonial challenge. The increasing evidence of regional disunity in Cambodia is a reflection of a centuries-old problem. The power accorded regional military commanders in Indonesia reflects the historical disunity of the Indonesian world more than the modern aim of 'Unity in Diversity'.

The image which emerges from an attempt to understand Southeast Asian revolts in historical terms will not be reassuring if reassurance is to be found in simple and optimistic terms. Rather it is an image of long-term risks of conflict with immense difficulties in the way of those who would lessen the risk of conflict. In substituting such a realistic vision of the future for the beguiling images of peace and progress one will come closer to understanding the true nature of Southeast Asia.

---

* For the singular importance of this simple but fundamental distinction I am indebted to discussion with Professor Harry J. Benda of Yale University.

B

# Chapter 2

# Traditional Patterns of Revolt

If the details of revolts in early Southeast Asian history are sparse, there is, nevertheless, abundant evidence of the frequency and the importance of these events. The revolts which are such a feature of Southeast Asia are readily classified in terms which are as applicable in Europe as in Asia. It is in their frequency and persistence that these revolts stress the slow progress of the Southeast Asian region towards the achievement of nation statehood. Without any pretence either to originality or to completeness, one might suggest that the traditional patterns of revolt in the Southeast Asian region are of four kinds or categories – at times these categories overlap or blend into each other.

Most easily identifiable are the revolts of captive peoples against an alien overlord. The tideflow of Southeast Asian history has resulted in the rise and fall of states and the expansion and contraction of their authority. The extension of authority by one state over another has, time and again, meant the emergence of resistance, frequently with mass support being joined to traditional leadership.

Revolt by one member of that traditional leadership against another provides a second classification. In recent years Western scholars have given increasing attention to the cosmological aspects of Southeast Asian kingship. In those states which sustained the impact of Indianization, so that their courts and administrations drew upon Indian models for guidance, the king became a semi-divine being. But it was always the office, rather than the man who held it, which was of utmost importance. The successful usurper gained or assumed the aura of his overthrown predecessor. With such high prestige attached to the office of king there had to be a justification for the success of the man who overthrew the ruler. In part this was supplied by the transferability of the aura of kingship, in part by the assumption that a usurped ruler must have himself violated established rules of conduct. With such justification available the opportunity for ambitious and able members of the elite to challenge their masters was considerable, and it should be no surprise that a change in ruler was so often achieved violently.

In Viet-Nam, the one state of Southeast Asia which sustained Sinic rather than Indian cultural influences, a different cosmology provided a similar justification. The passage of what has become loosely known as the 'mandate of heaven'* provided the opportunity to explain and legitimize the overthrow of the ruler. Only the assumption that this 'mandate' had truly passed from the ruler of Viet-Nam could justify the terrible break with Confucian values implied in the successful attack on the emperor.

Possibly the difference between the operation of these not dissimilar concepts in Indianized Southeast Asia and Sinic Southeast Asia lay in the contrast between individuals and dynasties. The Indianized states seem to have set less store by dynasties, so that the overthrow of an individual could come quite frequently. There was a significant recurrence of usurpations in Angkorian Cambodia, and in the Thai kingdoms that rose to power after the fall of the Angkorian empire. In these usurpations it was the man, not the dynasty, which fell, so that usurpers fabricated genealogies to link themselves with those whom they had defeated. In Viet-Nam, as in China, usurpation meant the end of a dynasty, not merely the end of a ruler's occupation of office.

The revolts of regions and of minorities have a long history in Southeast Asia. In some cases regional identifica-

* The Vietnamese term for this concept is *thien-menh*. The various connotations which attach to each of the two words making up the term, for instance 'heaven's decree' or 'divine direction', give it a much more powerful sense than can be implied in the now routine phrase 'mandate of heaven'.

tion and minority status combined. This was particularly the case for the upland groups who have come – so inaccurately – to be grouped under the single and excessively simple term *montagnards*. The term's inaccuracy is vividly demonstrated when one looks at an ethnic map of Southeast Asia, which delineates the rich geographical confusion of tribal groups within and across frontiers. The tension between hill and plain is a fundamental one in Southeast Asia and it has led to chronic conflict between plains dwellers and uplanders. Revolts have sprung, however, from other regions than the hills. The absence of strong central control of states in Southeast Asia has always carried with it the prospect of regional rebellion. Great officials in the outer regions of a loosely knit state have frequently seen little choice between the two extremes of a wide degree of untrammelled authority and armed defiance of the centre.

The final broad category is that of the 'millenarian' revolt. In Western societies which still find it necessary to accommodate an extraordinary number of fringe groups – bizarre religious sects and extremist political cliques – the persistent theme of millenarian revolt in the pre-modern societies of Southeast Asia should cause little surprise. Throughout recorded Southeast Asian history this thread may be traced. Inspired monks or individuals without formal religious status emerge as rallying points for movements which combine earthly aims with the promise of divine intervention or the assurance of miraculous rewards.

With revolts as such a persistent tradition in Southeast Asian history it would be an encyclopaedic task to attempt to list more than a fraction of those revolts which fall within the categories just enumerated. A few examples, deliberately chosen for their dramatic character or for their long-term significance, will amplify the distinctive features of these categories.

## Revolts Against Foreign Domination

The revolt of the Trung sisters in the first century AD has already been given passing attention. Their feats form part of the complex sense of national identity of all Vietnamese, whatever their political views. Detailed historical knowledge of their revolt against Chinese domination of what is now a section of North Viet-Nam is limited. It is clear that in AD 40 two Vietnamese sisters were involved in a revolt. The Vietnamese tradition is that one of the Trung sisters was a queen, the daughter of a general. With her younger sister she raised forces to attack the administrative centre of the region in which she lived, after the Chinese governor of the area had killed her husband. The countryside, tradition then recounts, rallied to her side to support her attacks on the hated Chinese foe. In response the Chinese emperor dispatched a leading general into Viet-Nam (or Giao-Chi as the then southernmost section of the Chinese empire was called) to confront the sisters. In AD 43 the Trung sisters led their troops against the Chinese, only to have the Vietnamese flee from superior force. The Trung, however, true to their aim of resisting those who had occupied their native land, threw themselves into a river and drowned.

The Chinese account of these events is, not surprisingly, different in both fact and perspective, justifying the execution of the elder sister's husband and giving little support to the suggestion of a popular and 'national' revolt. But even more interesting than the conflict between Vietnamese and Chinese tradition is the analysis which a distinguished twentieth century Vietnamese historian has made of the revolt. Bui Quang Tung has reviewed the various accounts of the sisters' defiance of China and suggested a quite different significance for the affair. The revolt against Chinese domination was, he believes, unsupported by the mass of the people. It involved a resistance to greater political control mounted by Chinese *émigrés* in Viet-Nam as well as by representatives of the old indigenous nobility. The failure of the assault on

# Region of Revolt

Chinese domination marked the moment when the Vietnamese elite accepted the necessity to adopt Chinese customs and civilization.

The account, enshrined in folklore, has survived as a reflection of the consistent Vietnamese resistance to foreign control. Revolt against alien political domination was of the first importance throughout Southeast Asian history. The capacity and the desire to manifest some national or regional identity through revolt was one of the indices of the survival and power of these identities. When historians write of the shattered state of Cambodia in the period shortly before the arrival of the French colonial presence, they should always be careful to qualify their comments by reference to the revolt against Vietnamese political control in the late 1830s and early 1840s. In those years the Vietnamese who occupied the shrunken kingdom of Cambodia found that even a population which had suffered as the Cambodians had held a sufficient sense of identity to resist the attempt to absorb them totally into Vietnamese society. The Cambodians were without their king and many of their traditional leaders were in exile in Bangkok, while others co-operated with the enemy. Despite these disadvantages, the Vietnamese interference in their lives and customs, and not least the efforts to undermine the prestige of the Cambodian Buddhist establishment, finally brought revolt. Some twenty years after the onset of this revolt the great Vietnamese mandarin Phan Thanh Gian could observe about Cambodia:

Our intention, in principle, is not at all to take over this country; we wish following heaven's example to leave these men to live and exist . . .

To some extent this was a pro-Vietnamese gloss on relations between Viet-Nam and Cambodia. Just as importantly, the observation reflected a Vietnamese realization of the capacity for resistance still present in Cambodia no matter how far, as French officials put it, she had 'fallen from her antique splendour'.

As the later, colonial, history of Southeast Asia shows, foreign domination was a constant spur for revolt. Whether linked with modern ideologies or associated with some quite traditional sense of national or regional identity, revolt against the alien is one of the most common, and the most successful of the appeals for action.

## Revolt Involving Elite Rivalries

The list of revolts which have pitted one member of a ruling group against another in the recorded history of Southeast Asia seems almost endless. The development of the modern Cambodian state might be fairly traced from the accession to power of Jayavarman II in the early decades of the ninth century when he, as a usurper – and possibly also as a leader of a national 'party' – unified various petty principalities into the Angkorian kingdom. We know little of the details of this development, or of the numbers who were involved in subsequent Angkorian history when other men rose to power by toppling the established monarch from the throne. Some of the most notable of the Angkorian rulers, Suryavarman I and Jayavarman VII, both reigning in the twelfth century, had to fight for their thrones.

The rise and fall of kingdoms and of leaders in early Javanese history reflects a similar continuing pattern of instability, with notable elite rivalry. As the distinguished English historian of Southeast Asia, Professor D. G. E. Hall, remarked in relation to the thirteenth century state of Singosari in eastern Java, 'The story of the early years of Singosari is completely lacking in details, save for the sordid list of murders through which one king was replaced by another.' The kingdom was founded by a usurper in 1222 and in the less than one hundred years of Singosari's existence as a state the throne was occupied by five men of whom three gained their thrones through usurpation.

In less ancient times there is more detail to be found of the still frequent instances in which one member of a

Southeast Asian ruling group rose up against another. Weak rulers or weak dynasties were an invitation to revolt. A case could be made for Cambodia, and possibly for other states in the region, to show that internecine struggle was more frequent in a direct relationship to the weakness of the state. As Cambodia's fortunes declined so were its princes more ready to struggle amongst themselves for the remnants of a once mighty kingdom. The constant human factors of ambition and rivalry found an ample range of material factors and external influences to trigger attempts at the sudden and violent overthrow of a rival. If there is nothing peculiarly Southeast Asian about such a situation – the history of Western Europe is, after all, punctuated by rivalry and revolt – the persistence and regularity of elite rivalry may provide a quantitative *and* qualitative difference. That elites should contend so frequently and so bitterly for power and resort to revolt in pursuit of their aim stresses the distinctive factor of inherent instability in states which lacked ethnic and regional unity, and a consensus as to the way in which power should pass from one ruler to another. Not least in the history of Southeast Asia one may see the difficult consequences of large royal families. As kings sired many sons by many wives they raised progeny who had little fraternal affection, but who were convinced, or brought to the conviction by ambitious advisers, that no one man's claim to the throne was better than another's. It was from such a situation that emerged the horrifying necessity for a new ruler to assure his position through a massacre of his kinsmen. In Burma and Thailand those princes who were seen as rivals risked being beaten to death with staves of sandalwood as they lay trussed up inside red velvet bags – a punishment that avoided the prohibition against the spilling of royal blood.

There were periods of calm in Southeast Asia and reigns that survived without challenge to the ruler's authority. These should be seen for what they were: the achievements of quite exceptionally strong rulers, often aided by external factors over which they had little real control, or the calm enforced by exhaustion. The calm which finally came to Viet-Nam in the late seventeenth century after one hundred years of battles reflected as much the exhaustion of the great seigneurial families of north and south as any final resolution of the question of who should control the whole of Viet-Nam. Strong rulers were insufficiently common in Southeast Asia and the factors for internal disunity were so great that it is not easy to find any sustained period of calm in which the threat or the fact of elite revolt was absent.

## The Revolts of Minorities and of Regions

The hill and padi dichotomy of Southeast Asia has been one of the most consistently important themes throughout the history of the countries in the area. Whatever the name attached to the hill peoples by their often more civilized neighbours in the plains, the connotation of the name has always been the same – 'savage'. The accuracy of this description has sometimes been doubtful. Certainly, many of the despised hill people had quite highly developed cultures. Moreover, the Mon-Khmer tribal groups to be found at a distance from the course of the Mekong River have a distinct affinity with their more developed lowland ethnic cousins. If racial myths were perpetuated which emphasized the distinctive differences between the people of the plain and those of the hills and mountains, it seems that there was much more passage between the two regions by individuals than was generally acknowledged. Professor E. R. Leach, writing about Burma, has pointed to the way in which an individual could be both a Kachin and a Shan, depending on the circumstances in which he found himself. The same opportunity appears to have been open for at least some of the 'savages'. They could, by conforming with the customs of the lowland, become lowlanders.

When the opportunities for such dual ethnic personality, or the passage from one socio-cultural group to another, is noted, however, it is the diverse nature of Southeast Asia's ethnic map which is so pronounced. What-

25

ever the nature of relations between these various communities – sometimes relations of long-term stability, at other times relations of bitter enmity – a sense of distinctiveness from ethnic group to ethnic group is one of the greatest historic features of the region. Modern maps and the existence of defined states too easily beguile us into forgetfulness of the complex ethnic rivalries of a large country such as Indonesia, or a small country such as Burma where independence has only accentuated the divisions between Burmans and the minority Shan, Chin, Kachin and Karen groups.

Given the preoccupations of the court chroniclers, it is not surprising that there are few details available of the revolts mounted by minority groups against their overlords. Revolt may be mentioned in the chronicles but without explanation of the cause of revolt or the problems inherent in minority-majority relationships. Viet-Nam provides an exception to this general observation. The Chinese tradition of court historiography has left more detail of the constant tension between the Vietnamese and the highland peoples. We know, for instance, of the very considerable difficulty which the great Vietnamese emperor Le Loi faced once he had expelled the Chinese forces which had occupied Viet-Nam at the beginning of the fifteenth century. Year after year he had to contend with resistance to the Vietnamese government from ethnically distinct Thai-speaking peoples within the boundaries which were claimed for the Vietnamese state.

Records are much fuller for revolts which matched Shans against Burmans, and Burmans against Mons. The turbulent history of Burma has been marked by a series of confrontations between ethnic groups. The conflict between the Burmans and the Mons – a people of great artistic capacity whose language has links with that of the Cambodians or Khmers – reached its final conclusion in the virtual destruction of the Mons as a distinct people in the nineteenth century. The hardier Shans came into conflict with the Burmans from the time of their entry into geographic Burma in force towards the end of the thirteenth century. As members of the great Thai-speaking linguistic family, the Shans were ethnic relatives of those peoples who had moved into the Menam valley to found principalities which were later united into Siam, or Thailand. The tragedy of Burma, at least in part, has lain in the efforts made both before and during the colonial period to develop a state which, by its ethnic composition, was predisposed against unity. Burmese history is marked by Shan resistance to and revolts against central control exercised by Burmans. The causes for revolt varied considerably from occasion to occasion. But whether the spur to action was excessive taxation or the thought that revolt might actually lead to a permanent end to Burmese political control, the fundamental fact of ethnic rivalry lay as a solid base on which to raise a revolt brought on by any number of immediate irritations.

While the revolt of minorities or of ethnically separate groups within Southeast Asian polities represents one of the most significant features of the endemic unrest of the region, due attention should be given to the fact that many revolts were mounted by members of the same ethnic group as a reflection of regional disenchantment with the central government. This fact emphasizes the general tendency among pre-colonial Southeast Asian states for relatively loose control by the centre over the outer regions. This was a situation of generally unresolved tension. Time and again central rulers had to choose between attempting to assert their power at the risk of open conflict with strong regional interests, or accepting that a regional leader would affirm allegiance only at the cost of considerable freedom from central control. In these circumstances only the strongest central rulers could exert their will over the whole of the state.

As one looks more closely at the history of Southeast Asia before the onset of colonial government it becomes abundantly clear that the states of the region were far from unified in terms which would have significance for those whose views of the nation or state stem from the European tradition. Possibly most dramatically, the Indonesian archipelago which was 'unified' under one independent government in the period after the Second World War was, essentially, a collection of states of widely varying size and power in the pre-colonial period. Indonesian claims of a great past in which the thirteenth and fourteenth century empire of Majapahit ruled over the regions currently within Indonesia's boundaries must be treated with the greatest reserve. It is undeniable that there were empires within the archipelago which did claim suzerainty over many of the states of pre-colonial times. What is open to debate is the extent of control which any suzerain claimed and exerted over his vassals.

That there should have been regional division and a mass of petty kingdoms in the Indonesian region accords easily with the size of that area and its island character. Where the existence of regional divisions and identity perhaps becomes more surprising or striking for the modern observer is in the mainland states of Southeast Asia. It is not only that we have become accustomed to the existence of such states as Viet-Nam, Thailand and Cambodia in modern times; there is sound historical evidence for the identifiable existence of these states over many centuries. Just because we know of the Angkorian state in Cambodia which described itself as 'Kambuja' (exactly the same term as that used by the current government in Phnom Penh) there is an immediate tendency to attribute to that earlier Kambuja the characteristics of a unified modern state. The same observation may be made about Thailand or about Viet-Nam. The concept of a unified Viet-Nam has, indeed, existed for centuries and has sustained Vietnamese resistance to foreign invasion; but the reality has often involved bitter division between sections of the country or between the court and the outer regions.

The great Vietnamese emperor Gia Long brought unity to the contending sections of his country in 1802. But this unity was fragile. The issue which caused fragility was not a result of any doubts on the part of Vietnamese about the existence of a separate and identifiable region known as Viet-Nam. One of the most striking of the historical themes in Viet-Nam has been the repeated assertion of a Vietnamese national identity. The problem which confronted Gia Long, and his successors before the French invasion of 1858, was how to reconcile regional tendencies in the north and south of his empire with the desire to assert control from the capital at Hue. Gia Long's own solution was to be reasonably liberal in his attitude towards the outer regions. Tax demands on the population of the far south of Viet-Nam were markedly less than was the case for those sections of the country where the imperial court's writ was more firmly established. The great eunuch general, Le Van Duyet, who had been one of Gia Long's most faithful and able companions in arms, was allowed to rule the Cochinchinese region of Viet-Nam with only a minimum of interference from Hue.* This situation was to change with Gia Long's death and the accession to the throne of his successor Minh Menh. Under the new ruler a stern effort was made to overcome regional differences. The outcome of the attempt to curtail the freedom which Cochinchina had enjoyed was the bitter Khoi revolt of 1833–5.

In some ways this revolt has become immortalized in the records of Vietnamese history for the wrong reasons. Generations of French scholars have taken note of the revolt by Le Van Khoi, the adopted son of Le Van Duyet, because it led to the cruelly prolonged death of a Catholic missionary who was captured with the rebels and to the execution of some hundreds of Vietnamese Christians in the slaughter which followed the capture of Saigon in 1835. The death of Father Marchand was one of the martyrdoms to which French Catholic opinion was able to appeal in the 1840s and 1850s, as increasingly strong efforts were made

* The term 'Cochinchina' is used here to designate the extreme south of Viet-Nam. It was the area which the French administered as the Colony of Cochinchina and is, very roughly, that section of Viet-Nam to the south of the Vietnamese Cordillera.

to involve the French Government in Vietnamese affairs. But the importance of the Khoi revolt, and its suppression, is not to be found in the record of Christian martyrdoms, whatever may be the truth of Father Marchand's involvement in the revolt. The collapse of the revolt was, much more profoundly, the resolution of a long-term problem in the Vietnamese state.

It is difficult to judge whether Gia Long had permitted the extreme south of his country a wide degree of freedom because he recognized the dangers of trying to force the region into the imperial mould, or whether his readiness to allow Le Van Duyet wide powers was a reward to one who had spent his life fighting for the emperor. The best assessment would take account of both these considerations. Gia Long seems to have sensed that this newly settled region of Viet-Nam could not be treated in the same way as those sections of the country in which settlement had been long established and formal administrative procedures had a substantial tradition.

In contrast to his father, the new emperor Minh Menh saw little reason for accepting regional differences within his state. He was reluctant to act against the greater freedom enjoyed by the administration in Cochinchina until the old general died; there is some evidence that he planned unsuccessfully to kill Le Van Duyet but failed. However, with the eunuch general's death, Minh Menh acted to administer Cochinchina on the same lines as the rest of Viet-Nam. New officials were dispatched to the south and the detailed pyramidal system of administration which Viet-Nam had adopted from China was applied. Such a change was too sudden for men who, like Le Van Khoi, had been used to the court at Hue playing a minimal role in the determination of daily administration. Led by Khoi, many of the officials joined together to resist Minh Menh and killed his newly dispatched administrators. This was a challenge which the emperor could not ignore and he suppressed it with all the fury of a man steeped in Confucian belief as to the rights and prerogatives of the ruler of the state. Conscious of the fate which lay in store for them, the rebels fought on against the superior numbers of the imperial troops until 1835, when the Saigon citadel was captured and over two thousand of its inhabitants put to the sword.

The end of the revolt marked the end of the southern region of Viet-Nam's quasi-independence from central administrative control. Minh Menh's success did not eliminate the sense of regional identity which continued, and continues, in southern Viet-Nam, but it defined the limits within which that regional identity should operate. The Khoi revolt marked the end of a period in Vietnamese history. From 1835 onwards, until the arrival of the French, the extreme south was increasingly brought into the web of Confucian practice both in education and administration. In the wider framework of the problem of revolt in Southeast Asia, the Khoi revolt was a notable demonstration of the readiness of regions, and regional officials, to fight for their position. The Nguyen dynasty which crushed the Khoi revolt was faced with revolt at the other extremity of its domains in the 1850s. Once again the interests of the centre and the outer regions were in conflict and revolt was the result.

## Millenarian Revolts

Heavy emphasis has already been placed on the way in which the records of Southeast Asian history before the advent of colonial administrations have as their preoccupations the doings of courts and kings. Because of this the assertion that millenarian revolts are a thread in the history of Southeast Asian societies must be made with singularly little proof. What proof one can muster is tentative and unsatisfactory. It is tantalizing to find in a version of the Cambodian Chronicle the statement that:

In 1730, a Laotian from the village of Prea Sot on the edge of the province of Baphnom became inspired. He announced that he was invested with a superhuman power and that he was going to use it to exterminate the Vietnamese who did not cease to harm Cambodia. This adventurer or madman was, however, able to unite about him credulous people. He knew how to inspire them with great confidence and because of this he was able to wage war in the very territory of Viet-Nam ...

Why did the population of this province accept the leadership of such an individual? The answer almost certainly is to be found in terms of their expectation that such an 'inspired' leader would transform their world, bringing a new era in which the demands of the present would be satisfied and rich unreal promises of the future fulfilled.

While much uncertainty must attach to the incidence of millenarian revolts in which leaders claiming special insights and powers rallied peasants to follow them in revolt against established authority, there should be little doubt about their existence. In part this lack of doubt is a result of our more detailed (but still far from satisfactory) knowledge of millenarian movements in more recent times. Unless one assumed that the millenarian movements of the colonial period emerged *sui generis*, and unless one argues that in the pre-colonial period the Southeast Asian peasant was not subject to pressures which could only be relieved by adhesion to a movement claiming a supernatural capacity to change the world, one cannot dismiss the existence of a long history of millenarian movements. Our knowledge of the daily life of a Southeast Asian peasant in the pre-colonial period is sadly limited and must be based to a considerable extent on retrospective application of modern models. Nevertheless, the court chronicles make it clear that life for the peasant could be difficult in the extreme. Across the east-west boundaries of the mainland Southeast Asian states lay regions which became marching grounds for rival armies. The lot of a peasant in such an area was unenviable. The 'Monland' region of modern southern Burma and the western area of modern Cambodia about Pursat province were devastated time and again. Colonial administrators recorded bitter memories of destruction visited upon those villages and towns which had lain along traditional invasion routes before colonial governments instituted their passing era of peace.

For disoriented peasants the sudden appearance of a monk who claimed divine revelation which would enable him to institute a golden age, once he and his followers had overthrown the existing government, could spark a sudden surge of revolt. Credulous peasants would accept the assurances that magical practices rendered them invulnerable and march against the provincial capital, frequently to be butchered by the better armed troops of their overlord.

The historian must rely on sociologists and anthropologists for deeper study of the factors involved in the emergence of millenarian and messianic movements, and on a thorough study of the often detailed accounts which are provided of such movements in colonial archives before a more satisfactory picture emerges of these movements' importance. For the moment it is sufficient to record their existence and to recognize that Southeast Asian peasants plagued by war, taxes and omnipresent death from unexplained causes would, on occasion, react through participation in millenarian movements, which involved revolt against established authority.

For the pre-colonial period in the history of Southeast Asian states the record of revolts, inspired by whatever cause or combination of causes, is frequently so limited as to prevent any detailed examination. Yet the record is not so sparse nor the details so barren as to prevent some valid generalizations of the sort attempted in this chapter. Above all is the general view of Southeast Asia which emerges as an area fraught with factors of instability. The revolts which broke out in later periods belong to their own time, by definition, but they do not represent a total break with the past. In the revolts of the era of colonial domination and beyond, the importance of traditional factors may be discerned beneath, and sometimes alongside, the gloss of immediate cause and motivation.

c

# Chapter 3

# Tradition in a Colonial Context

The European newcomer did not bring forth revolts as a new concept in those regions of Southeast Asia which became his colonies. Viet-Nam had demonstrated its resistance to Chinese rule in the pre-colonial period. Even a shattered Cambodia, shrunken to a mere residuum of its former population, turned on the Vietnamese who occupied the country in the late 1830s. But if the problems posed by an alien presence were not new, and if the response to that alien presence had a long history of precedents, there was already a qualitative change once Southeast Asians mounted revolts against European colonial overlords. The gap between the technology of the European and the Southeast Asian has remained marked into the twentieth century. The Southeast Asian who rose in revolt had to contend with the dismaying fact that weight of numbers and an overwhelming belief in the rightness of a cause did not assure success against those who fought with more advanced weaponry and their own conviction in both the rectitude and necessity of their presence in a foreign land.

Yet even taking account of this early qualitative change, the major watershed in any consideration of the revolts of the colonized against those who were their rulers was reached when tradition was supplanted by a new vision of the future. The early anti-colonial revolts were led by men accustomed to stand at the head of the peasantry and to lead them into battle. Traditional leaders and their traditional officials led revolts against colonial masters with the hope of recapturing the values of the past – a past untransformed by the modernist introductions of alien culture, and certainly not marked by any change in the relationship between the peasants of the 'little tradition' and the courts and officials of the 'great tradition' of Asia. The watershed was crossed when men looked to the future rather than to the past, despite the continuance in leadership positions of men who had sprung from the traditional ruling class. Nevertheless, if some time during the twentieth century tradition was supplanted by programmatic ideologies which urged revolt because of virtues of the future rather than the past, such a development did not mean that tradition had entirely vanished. Resistance to foreign dominion is a theme in Southeast Asian revolt which is timeless.

Indeed, to speak of a 'watershed' may be a misleading metaphor. Not only do aspects of tradition remain in the modern, programmatic revolts of the twentieth century: the passage from the period in which tradition in all its forms was dominant to that time when visions of the future rather than the past become more important is no simple movement over a single barrier. The image of a watershed is correct only so long as a series of interlocking valleys and foothills is included on either side of, and even intersecting, the central spine of the mountain range. Before the modernist elements in anti-colonial revolts became dominant, resistance movements had wended their way through a situation in which tradition and modernity appeared to be balanced, one against the other.

Tradition was not only present in anti-colonial revolts in the form of leadership by men of the old ruling class seeking a return to an earlier system of government. The tradition of millenarian uprisings, if this too may be called a tradition, was abundantly apparent. It was almost as if the technological superiorities of the European colonizer encouraged the emergence of movements which put their faith in magical power to achieve fantastic aims. Throughout mainland Southeast Asia the history of anti-colonial revolts is marked by reports of poorly armed men who charged against the modern weapons of their colonial rulers, convinced that magic had made them invulnerable.

One of the best known instances of this futility was an occasion in Burma at the end of the nineteenth century, when a handful of Burmans stormed an English club which had once formed part of the royal palace, convinced that to capture the palace would be to ensure becoming ruler of Burma. The attackers believed they were invulnerable, but well placed shots from hunting rifles handled by the club members showed they were not. For every instance of revolt which has been widely reported there are several which have passed out of notice. Claims of invulnerability formed an important aspect of one of the least known of anti-colonial revolts in the nineteenth century, the Cambodian Rising of 1885–6. Better known, if still awaiting detailed research, was the Saya San revolt of 1930 and 1931 in Burma, in which, once again, men took no account of the odds against them because of their conviction that specially invoked magical powers would protect them.

No single book could list in any detail the multitude of revolts which erupted during the colonial period in Southeast Asia. For many of these revolts the published accounts are limited in their details and biased in their attitudes. For others, only the briefest mention in public documents may hide the existence of much material still awaiting investigation in the archives. In other cases, the details of anti-colonial revolts have largely passed out of memory, forgotten both by the citizens of the country in which the revolts took place and by the descendants of those colonial officials and soldiers who found themselves fighting strange wars in a strange land. In this latter category is the Pahang 'War' 1891–5, which provides one of the few recorded examples of Malay resistance to the British forward movement into the Malayan Peninsula during the last three decades of the nineteenth century. It was no major rising, yet it required the British to commit some five hundred military police in Pahang before the affair was terminated in 1895 after months of sporadic fighting. The Pahang 'War' has seldom occupied more than a page in a general history of Malaya, yet it and the outbreaks of peasant violence which occurred in Trengganu and Kelantan in the twentieth century provide the long-neglected evidence that the Malays were not so markedly different in their reaction to the changes brought by the onset of foreign control as has been usually supposed.

Two well known anti-colonial revolts, the Java War of the 1820s and the Scholars' Revolt in Viet-Nam in the 1880s, and one neglected revolt, the Cambodian Rising of the 1880s, provide excellent examples of movements led by traditional leaders against a colonial power. Set in different countries and emerging from different cultures, each has the fundamental similarity of being backward looking, a fact which, whatever the interpretations given them by modern nationalist historians, makes them preeminently traditional in tone.

## The Java War

Javanese mythology has interwoven through its complex cosmology the belief in a 'liberating prince' who in periods of difficulty for his people would emerge to rout the oppressor and bring his followers into a golden age. Such a belief is linked not so much with the Islamic religion (which historically was a latecomer to the inland principalities of central and eastern Java) as with older indigenous beliefs which had blended with religious and philosophic concepts derived from India. Many men have been regarded in their own time as fulfilling the role of the liberator. King Airlangga, who in the eleventh century restored a Javanese empire out of chaos, was perhaps the most widely revered of the liberator figures who were to emerge over the centuries before Prince Diponegoro led his followers against the Dutch in the Java War which lasted from 1825 to 1830. In our own time, part of the undoubted charisma which surrounded President Sukarno in his days of power stemmed from a popular belief that he too could fill the role of the liberator.

Whatever the nationalist qualities assigned to Prince

Diponegoro in the twentieth century, his decision to rise in revolt against the Dutch cannot be understood unless due attention is given to the motivation of his frustrated ambitions. As a result both of the complex requirements of Javanese customary law and of decisions taken by Thomas Stamford Raffles during the period when Britain ruled in Java, Prince Diponegoro had been passed over when succession to the throne of the principality of Jogjakarta was determined. This decision left Diponegoro an embittered man.

In the early nineteenth century the ruler of Jogjakarta had little real freedom of action, but he retained great significance for his people as the representative on earth of the cosmic powers which controlled the universe. The Dutch had recognized the significance of the relationship between the Sultan of Jogjakarta and his people and had chosen to rule through him. Thus, while his power was limited, a ruler of Jogjakarta commanded the loyalty of his people and believed, himself, in the cosmic importance of his position. That Diponegoro should have been disappointed not to succeed to the throne in these circumstances is no surprise. A follower of Islam, he was an adept of pre-Islamic religious techniques, fasting in the wilderness and meditating in caves. Such a man was a fearsome opponent for the Dutch when he chose to rise in revolt. He claimed to be the rightful ruler of the state who had been prevented from gaining the throne only by the infidel Europeans. Diponegoro was a devout Muslim, and at the same time a man whose way of life was recognizable by the Javanese peasants as similar to that led by great royal mystics in the distant pre-Islamic past.

There is abundant evidence to show that revolts are complex affairs, and that leadership, however able and however tinged with charisma, can make no headway if other elements are not present. Such elements were present in Diponegoro's case. His ability to summon support reflected the cosmic virtues which others saw in his person, but this was not all. Just as importantly, his call to revolt came at a period in Javanese history when a variety of decisions by the Dutch colonial government had led to widespread discontent and resentment among both the peasantry and the traditional officials. Indeed, it was the latter whose support was most important for Diponegoro and whose financial prospects had been severely restricted in the years just before the outbreak of the Java War. Dutch rule had reduced the territory under the control of the ruler of Jogjakarta, and so reduced the opportunities for court officials to place their relatives and retainers on land which could provide them with income and sustenance. Shortly before the outbreak of the revolt the situation had been made even more unsatisfactory for the Javanese chiefs when contracts which they had negotiated with foreigners for the use of their land were cancelled by the Dutch. With their economic interests at stake, the traditional aristocracy had material grievances to add to their spiritual convictions.

For the peasantry economic hardships may have been of a less acute sort, but there is no doubt that they too had grievances which played a part in their readiness to revolt. The Dutch had placed the right to levy highway tolls in the hands of Chinese concessionaires who battened upon the Javanese traveller. The general problem of disorientation in a period of rapid change seems to have been present also. In the case of the Java War, as with other areas of Southeast Asia, this atmosphere of disorientation reinforced the power of the traditional elite to command a following amongst the peasantry when the time came to revolt.

The spark that lit the fires of revolt was a dispute between Diponegoro and the Dutch over a road which the colonial authorities sought to build over land containing a sacred tomb. With a band of his closest followers Diponegoro established himself in dissidence in the mountains close to Jogjakarta and from there proceeded to wage a guerrilla warfare campaign of the type so characteristic of revolts in Southeast Asia, in which an inferior force enjoying some popular support faces a technologically superior enemy. The final result of Diponegoro's efforts was his treacherous seizure by the Dutch after he had agreed to meet with them to discuss an end to the war. This came, however, when there was no hope that he could prevail militarily over the increasingly large numbers of troops opposed to him.

The disruption caused by the Java War and the staggering cost in lives provide the indices of how serious the affair was as a challenge to Dutch authority. Fifteen thousand troops of the Dutch colonial forces were lost in the campaign, more than half of them Dutchmen. Upwards of two hundred thousand peasants died in the five-year course of the war, most of them from the resulting food shortages and diseases which the campaign brought. That Diponegoro could resist capture and trouble the Dutch for such a long period reflected many of the factors which were essential for the successful mounting, if not conclusion, of anti-colonial revolts. He, and some of his lieutenants, proved to be guerrilla leaders of considerable talent. Fighting in an area which they and their followers knew well, they had these essential advantages over those who were sent against them. As a traditional leader who was credited with cosmic powers and with particular devotion to Islam, Diponegoro's appeals to the peasants in the Jogjakarta region came from a man who almost better than any other was likely to arouse support and loyalty. And when those appeals were made to peasants and aristocrats who could ascribe the difficulties of a changing environment to the easily identifiable Dutch foreigners, the prospects for revolt were high.

But Diponegoro failed. Deserted by his closest followers and betrayed into exile in Sulawesi, his revolt had been a brave show of defiance. At no stage did it seem likely to force the Dutch from Java, or even a section of it. With the support of the population Diponegoro had demonstrated what opportunities for resistance lay beneath the surface calm of relations between the Javanese and the

Dutch. But this was not enough for success. His revolt was firmly rooted in tradition and offered no new earthly paradise, whatever blessings might have been attached to death as the result of involvement in a holy war against the Dutch infidels.

## The Scholars' Revolt in Viet-Nam

Modern Indonesian nationalist propagandists have seen Diponegoro as a nationalist figure when historical accuracy would more correctly place him as a regional leader in a traditional framework. In contrast, there is at least room for debate over the existence of nationalism in the Vietnamese Scholars' Revolt which broke out in 1885 and dragged on, in a much diminished form, for more than a decade afterwards. If 'nationalism' is defined in terms which stress modern concepts of the nation state, then there can be no suggestion that the Scholars' Revolt was nationalistic in character. What the revolt did possess was an undoubted national identification. Through the long recorded history of the independent Vietnamese state, the existence of a national identification has been one of the most consistent themes in the development of the country. Regional divisions were always important and these were sometimes intensified by political division. Yet despite geographic and administrative differences between the regions of Viet-Nam the ideal of a single Viet-Nam was preserved among the population. When the French arrived as colonialists in the middle of the nineteenth century, it was as Vietnamese first, and not as men from one region or another of the country, that the mandarins and their soldiers resisted the invaders.

With a history of national identification widespread amongst the population the failure of the Vietnamese court to resist the French colonial advance remains one of the more puzzling aspects of Viet-Nam's modern history. Part of the answer undoubtedly lies in the personality of the Vietnamese ruler at the time of the French advance. The Emperor Tu Duc was at heart a scholar who was beset by indecision when considerations of an urgent practical nature demanded his attention. His military mandarins fought bravely against the French in the early years of the colonial period but they were unable to contend with the better armed French soldiers. From 1861 to 1885 the court had to accept a slow French extension of control. First the French had gained three of the six provinces in Cochinchina; then the remaining three provinces were taken over to make the whole of the rich south of Viet-Nam a French colony. After French false starts in the 1870s, the years 1883 and 1884 saw the institution of a French protectorate over the remaining northern and central sections of Viet-Nam and so the end to Viet-Nam's tenuously preserved independence. The year 1883 had also been marked by Tu Duc's death. This event had led to the Vietnamese throne being occupied in quick succession by three weak young princes until a further young prince aged twelve, Ham Nghi, was placed on the throne in 1884 by the men who had become the real powers in the Vietnamese court. These were the regents Ton That Thuyet and Nguyen Van Tuong. Of these two men, Ton That Thuyet was an implacable enemy of the French. He argued for armed revolt against the French and the young ruler agreed with his proposal.

The plan miscarried. Ton That Thuyet's intention had been to liquidate the French garrison which was quartered in the Vietnamese imperial city at Hue. When this proved impossible, Thuyet and Ham Nghi, accompanied by those mandarins who had long regretted the subservient position which the Vietnamese court had adopted, fled into the mountain fastnesses in the west of Viet-Nam. Moving his headquarters frequently, Thuyet, as the practical, but not the symbolic, leader of the resistance, organized the guerrilla operations which were the only means open to the Vietnamese of fighting on anything approaching equal terms with the French. The response to Ham Nghi's appeals for support and to Thuyet's organizational efforts was remarkable. The long years of indecisive hesitation by Tu Duc and his court had bred a desire for action on the part of many of the Vietnamese official class throughout northern and central Viet-Nam. So long as Tu Duc lived, there was a moral inhibition against any attempt to strike at either the symbols or substance of French power in southern Viet-Nam. And even after Tu Duc's death, while the three weak youths who preceded Ham Nghi sat briefly upon the throne at Hue, the mandarins who lacked an imperial sanction were reluctant to act against the French, who now had extended their control over all Viet-Nam. Although Ham Nghi's departure from Hue was a break with one of the most important instances of state symbolism which demanded the emperor's almost constant presence in the imperial city, it was as emperor that he called for revolt. His brother, who had been given the throne after Ham Nghi's flight, was enthroned with appropriate ceremony, but his appeal as emperor was only to those who were prepared to accept a policy of collaboration.

Despite the fact that the revolt which began in 1885 has been widely known as the Scholar's Revolt, Vietnamese historians make a distinction between the phase of anticolonial resistance which had Ham Nghi as its rallying symbol and the resistance which continued after Ham Nghi's capture in 1888. The same men were involved in fighting against the French in the second phase, but after 1888 the mandarins and the people fought on without any hope that their actions would bring change to Viet-Nam through support of the man who had been king. This distinction is an important one if we can accept, as some Vietnamese historians strongly maintain, that amongst the men who fought in the closing phases of the resistance which began in 1885 there were those who had begun to think beyond resistance to revolution. If this assertion is too strong, in the light of rather problematical evidence, there is no doubt that many men who had fought in the earlier Scholars' Revolt went on, in later years, to become members of resistance movements which were quite certainly modernist in outlook. For the moment the division of resistance into a Royalist and then a Scholars' phase highlights the determination of many Vietnamese in the 1880s to fight on against the French when the odds lay heavily against them, and despite the fact that a royal leader was no longer at the head of their movement.

The traditionalist element was dominant in both phases of this revolt. Ham Nghi's proclamation to rally support which he issued in 1885 is full of classical allusions and couched in terms which assert the emperor's ultimate authority. The Regent Thuyet sought no basic change in the pattern of Vietnamese life, nor any concession to changing times. He had encouraged revolt in order to return to what had been. After the emperor had been captured and his older adviser had fled to China in 1888, those who continued to resist the French justified their positions in much the same terms as had been used before. The country was invaded, as it had been centuries before by the Chinese, and it was every Vietnamese person's duty to fight against those who trampled upon Viet-Nam's sovereignty. The revolt had been led by the ruler and his forced exile did not change the fact that resistance was on behalf of the Vietnamese royal house as it had been enshrined in Ham Nghi. While French politicians in Paris spoke of the swift success of schemes for pacification, stubborn Vietnamese guerrilla groups held out for years before superior French force slowly ground them down. Anti-guerrilla tactics described in such familiar terms for the modern reader as the 'oil spot technique' were pronounced by French generals to be the answer to continuing Vietnamese resistance. But the achievement of French success was slow indeed.

As the prelude to a changed outlook amongst those Vietnamese who resisted the French, the revolt which began in 1885 was of signal importance. The revolt's ultimate failure not only forced educated Vietnamese to reassess the techniques of warfare which had proved inadequate; in addition it forced them to make an intellectual reassessment of the aims for which they fought. The revolt with its royalist and then scholars' phases had no real answer to the present except in terms of the past; an ideal rather than an actual past. That the past should include major elements which were to continue throughout Vietnamese anti-colonial movements of the twentieth century does not invalidate this observation. The nature of Vietnamese history had developed a sense of national identification and the widely held ideal of a single independent Vietnamese state. This sense of identity and the ideal perception of what Viet-Nam should be were the timeless elements which joined with new philosophies in later years. In the revolts which were so bravely but ineffectively promoted after 1885 these elements formed part of a matrix of ideas clearly attuned to the past.

## The Cambodian Rising of 1885–6

The Java War came to be a symbol for Indonesian nationalists as the first anti-colonial revolt of a movement which finally achieved its aims through revolution after the Second World War. The Vietnamese Scholars' Revolt was closely followed by new anti-French movements in the almost ceaseless record of resistance to the colonial power. The events in both Java and Viet-Nam were given considerable publicity in their own period and are well known as part of the history of resistance which is treasured today. In very considerable contrast, the Cambodian Rising which broke out in 1885 and lasted through 1886 received remarkably little attention in contemporary French accounts of developments in that prized section of their colonial empire, 'notre Indochine'. Moreover, until very recently the great majority of Cambodians had only a very limited memory of an event which both in its magnitude and significance was of the first importance to their country's history. Whereas French military histories dismissed the Cambodian Rising as a minor inconvenience, the records preserved in the French and Cambodian Archives tell of an affair involving as many as ten thousand

Cambodians fighting against nearly five thousand French-led troops. The documents in the archives suggest that as many as ten thousand people died as a result of the disruption caused by the Rising and make it clear that one of the notable results of the affair was the mass emigration of Cambodians out of the west of their country into the more peaceful provinces which had once been Cambodian but which were controlled by Siam during the nineteenth century.

The Cambodian Rising was the only major anti-colonial revolt mounted against the French during the history of the French Protectorate in Cambodia. When the Protectorate was instituted in 1863 the French had acted with little other thought than to protect their interests in the newly acquired colony of Cochinchina. Over the years, however, French interest in Cambodia grew, and with this interest came a determination to transform the government of King Norodom, the great grandfather of the former Cambodian Chief of State, Prince Sihanouk. It was this desire to limit Norodom's power which brought about the Rising.

Norodom's own resentment of limitations on his freedom of action and the resentment felt by his senior officials concerning French treatment both of the king and of their own interests led to a widespread revolt. Here, again, the essential character of the revolt was traditionalist. As was the case in Viet-Nam, in the revolts taking place at the same period, the Cambodian officials who took part in this Rising had some sense of a national identity. But the revolt was not nationalist if that term is meant to imply a forward looking transformation of the country. Cambodia in the late nineteenth century was far from a nation state in which the population in general had both the sense of belonging to the state and the opportunity to participate in the decision-making which guided its destinies.

The Cambodian peasant's ultimate loyalty was to his king. Yet if that ruler did not protect him from the frequently avaricious officials, the peasant felt no qualms about crossing his country's frontiers to live under the control of another government.

When the fires of revolt broke out in January 1885 they arose from many scattered embers of resentment and apprehension. The principal cause of the revolt can be identified in the clash of personalities which resulted when King Norodom faced the demand by Charles Thomson, the French Governor of Cochinchina with responsibility for Cambodia, that he should give up those regal powers of government which he had preserved through the first twenty years of the French Protectorate. This was a demand which no previous French official had been prepared to force on Norodom. Although Frenchmen had deplored Norodom's way of life and his attitude to government, they had also recognized the importance of the king within the Cambodian state and the likelihood that a real challenge to the king would bring in its train a widespread outbreak of resistance to their control exercised through the Protectorate. In June 1884 Thomson forced King Norodom to sign a convention which stripped the king of power. Norodom signed under duress with French gunboats moored in the Mekong River off his palace and only after he had found that his delaying actions were to no avail. Whatever other motivations became involved in the Rising, it was the signature of the convention and the assault which this document represented on the king's power which was the principal rallying point throughout the resistance which the Cambodians raised against the French.

Still unclear in the very considerable evidence which has accumulated about the Rising is the extent to which direction and organization of the affair came from the king. Cambodians who do remember the Rising have assigned a leading role in its organization to Norodom. The French during the revolt were similarly convinced that Norodom was closely involved, but they could never produce hard evidence to justify this belief. Certainly, even if the evidence available is only implicit and circumstantial, there is every reason to believe that Norodom was aware of plans for the Rising and followed its development closely. Once resistance to the French had broken out in one region of Cambodia further troubles quickly developed elsewhere. In the east of the kingdom the resentment felt by officials against the treatment of their king by the French was matched by popular resentment against the way in which the French Protectorate had led to the introduction of large numbers of the hated Vietnamese into Cambodian territory. In the south and southwest the long resistance of bands led by traditional officials suggests that concern for the king was matched by concern for the way in which French control of government would undermine their own position. The whole affair was further complicated by the emergence, as a leading guerrilla leader, of the king's half brother, Prince Si Votha. This prince had been in dissidence against the king for twenty years. Now, he claimed, his efforts were directed solely against the French. The truth of his claim is doubtful, but there is clear evidence that he rallied his followers in terms of the French treatment of the king.

Militarily the development of the Cambodian Rising provided an almost classic illustration of the difficulties faced by alien forces in a small war situation. The insurgents knew the countryside and the French troops – both Frenchmen and their colonial troops from Viet-Nam and North Africa – did not. With rare exceptions the Cambodians fought against the French in small bands, shooting only from behind cover and fading away when superior numbers approached. Although most of the support which the insurgents received appears to have come voluntarily, the Cambodian guerrillas were in a much better position than the French to coerce the peasant population where this was necessary. French reports are only too ready to admit that sealing off villages from the insurgents was an impossibility. While the French flying columns could make their presence felt whenever they ventured out of their secure positions it became clear by the end of 1885 that unless French troops were on the ground, the insurgents would prevail in unpatrolled areas. And prevail they did with constant attacks against any who could be identified as associates of the French, including Catholic missionaries and Chinese tax farmers. Some major French posts were under almost total siege for upwards of twelve months as Cambodians, spurred on by their traditional leaders and on occasion by inspired mystics who promised invulnerability, roamed unchallenged through the countryside.

The way in which the Rising ended emphasizes its essentially traditional character. Slowly a realization grew in French official minds that there could be no end to the Rising so long as Norodom remained unappeased. With great effort on the part of the French to save face an approach was finally made to Norodom which called for his assistance in ending the Rising in return for French restraint in their application of the 'reforms' introduced by the 1884 convention. In his proclamation calling for an end to the Rising, Norodom made clear that it was the French challenge to Cambodian traditions and usages which had been the cause of the revolt. To the force of his written call for an end of the fighting Norodom added his personal prestige as he travelled into some of the most disturbed regions of his kingdom. In these visits tradition was paramount, as Norodom called for loyalty to his decision from those who had been fighting against the French as part of the general loyalty which was owed the king.

The Cambodian Rising, which drew swiftly to a close when the king was persuaded to work for peace, was the one great challenge which Cambodians offered French power before the period of general decolonization in Southeast Asia in the years after 1946. Its traditional nature left no new thought for revolutionaries to build upon in their search for change. Indeed, the successful manipulation of Cambodian dynastic rivalries by the French Protectorate in subsequent years ensured that for the first four decades of the twentieth century the Cam-

D

bodian throne was occupied by men who were unready to challenge French interests in their country. These later years of peace have dimmed the memory of the Rising, but it was of a size and a nature to deserve the attention which historians have begun to accord it. Overwhelmingly traditional in tone, the Rising nevertheless had something of the quality of being all things to all men. It could provide the opportunity for the emergence of mystics who promised invulnerability and it could lead to action against alien Vietnamese whose infiltration into Cambodia was so deeply resented. The Rising strengthened the will of traditional officials who feared that the French presence in the kingdom was about to limit their powers and advantages, but it also could bring them to demonstrate the loyalty and devotion which they accorded a ruler who remained a semi-divine being.

The three revolts just considered were traditional in their aims and in their approaches to the implementation of those aims. The peasants who were recruited to fight on behalf of Norodom or Diponegoro did not have the prospect of a new form of state held up to them as an incentive. The Vietnamese mandarins who came out of retirement in response to the edicts issued in Ham Nghi's name reacted to the summons in terms of their Confucian view of the state in which it was their duty to obey. These were the exact sentiments of one man who had no hesitation in abandoning one Confucian virtue, that of mourning for his dead mother, to fulfil another and higher virtue, that of serving his emperor.

In the case of the Java War there is difficulty in discerning national identity, let alone nationalism. But for the revolts in Viet-Nam and Cambodia the element of national identity must be admitted. The Java War was a regional revolt. The appeal to regionalism, or to identity with the principality of Jogjakarta, may have involved many of the same components which later made up Indonesian nationalism, and indeed may have provided an important basis for later nationalism. Through their relatively limited size and their history the Vietnamese and Cambodian states in the nineteenth century had already developed some sense of national identity. This was to form an important part of the later development of nationalism in both countries, but national identity did not forge one single nationalism for Viet-Nam, nor fan an active nationalism into life in Cambodia in the peaceful years before the Second World War. Because of the strong traditional tone of the revolts which have been described, and of similar revolts in other areas, the transition to revolts in which non-traditional elements were paramount could not come quickly. And even with those elements assuming a major importance it would be dangerously simple to exclude from one's understanding of these new situations an appreciation of the continuing theme of rejection of foreign control of Southeast Asian destinies.

# Chapter 4

## Seed Time of Revolt:
## The Years Before the
## Second World War

Historically, Southeast Asian countries have absorbed new ideas from the outside world rather than diffused their own indigenous beliefs through the regions which border the area. The Buddhist countries of Southeast Asia and the states which controlled the Indonesian Archipelago and the Malayan Peninsula were profoundly affected by Indian thought and religion; and Islam subsequently came to play a role of great importance in the maritime regions. What has been called the 'Hispanization' of the Philippines is a reflection of the extent to which the long Spanish occupation of that country has affected its cultural patterns. Viet-Nam, alone among the countries of Southeast Asia, absorbed the culture of China, so that the Vietnamese court modelled itself and its administration on the Confucian-dominated system of a country whose political control it resisted.

This absorption of external influences has never meant that Southeast Asian countries are without their own indigenous beliefs and their own culture. Nor have the external influences while slowly taking root remained unchanged in their new setting. Indeed, one eminent scholar has pointed out that even in the earliest times, when Indian culture came to Southeast Asia at the very beginning of the Christian era, it must be assumed that Southeast Asians were already sophisticated enough to recognize the value and utility of a complex alien culture, and capable of shaping that culture in their own way.

This long history of cultural borrowing must be remembered when one comes to consider the growth of nationalist movements and the emergence of new forms of resistance to colonial rule which developed in the twentieth century. Faced with the political dominance of their colonial governments, those Southeast Asians who wished to change their condition looked outside the region to examples which showed how Asians could defeat Europeans or which demonstrated the power of new political philosophies to transform old patterns of life. The example of Japan had a powerful effect on the thought of Southeast Asians at the beginning of the twentieth century. Even before the success of the Japanese in the Russo-Japanese War of 1904–5, Vietnamese who were unready to accept indefinite rule by the French had begun to look at the changes which were taking place in Japan. The Japanese capacity to combine industrial modernization with the preservation of traditional cultural values was particularly attractive to men who held revolutionary ideas, in terms of their wish to overthrow colonial rule, but who still were deeply committed to the cultural system of their own country. When the Japanese did triumph in their war with the Russians, this Asian success was greeted by politically conscious Southeast Asians – still a desperately small number of persons – as both a vindication of their hopes and an encouragement for the future.

If the Japanese victory over the Russians was important in providing a new degree of confidence amongst Southeast Asians who questioned the right of the colonial powers to rule, the Chinese and Russian revolutions were of even greater significance. Out of both these revolutions, the first taking place in 1911 and the second in 1917, came political ideas which are still of the deepest importance for the Southeast Asian region. The most dramatic of the revolts against colonial domination in Viet-Nam have been led by men who had found basic answers in Marxism. The drama of the Nghe-An Soviets of 1930, in which the Vietnamese peasantry was first successfully organized to resist the French, will always capture our attention. So too will the 1926–7 Communist revolts in Indonesia remain as a fascinating but almost incredible example of mistiming and mismanagement. The Malayan Emergency which

53

developed after the Second World War and the Huk challenge to the Philippines state were again mounted by men who were Communists.

But ideas other than Communism played their part in the slow development of mass opposition to colonial rule. The stress on nationalist identity which had been so much a part of the Chinese revolution found a ready response in the minds of Southeast Asian politicians. Later, the social democratic ideas of Europe and the political philosophies of the growing Indian nationalist movement became important. Just because Marxist leadership has been at the heart of some of the most notable and dramatic instances of revolt against colonial rule in Southeast Asia, it is easy to overlook the fact that only in one state of the region has a Communist government come to power. It is not by chance that only in this one country, Viet-Nam, has nationalism become so indissolubly joined with Communism. The difficulties involved in applying Marxist concepts to societies of Southeast Asia provides part of the explanation for Viet-Nam's unique position. More positively, the capacity of non-Communist leaders in Southeast Asia to convince their followers that there are alternatives to Communism has been important, particularly when these leaders have had a firm grip on all significant military power. In anything less than the most detailed study of Viet-Nam one risks excessive simplification in attempting to describe any particular situation or development. Nevertheless, it is difficult to argue with the conclusion that only in Viet-Nam was the combination of colonial repression and skilful Communist leadership such as to lead to the latter's success. In other countries the extent of repression varied, but, with the possible exception of Indonesia, the non-Communists were never so consistently hamstrung in their efforts to achieve political advancement. Only in Viet-Nam, finally, was a colonial power of the Southeast Asian region prepared to fight to the bitter end in its efforts to prevent independence.

There is a constant risk in discussing the countries of

Southeast Asia of giving the impression of a region in which similarities are considerably more important than differences. There is much that is common to Southeast Asia, but seldom can too much stress be given to the individual experience of each country. When one points to the external influences which had importance throughout the Southeast Asian region, no less importance should be accorded to the different ways in which the Southeast Asian states reacted to those influences.

The years before the Second World War were by no means universally troubled ones in the region. Nor were the revolts which took place all cast in the same mould. Dramatic revolts took place in both Viet-Nam and Indonesia which were inspired, for their leaders at least, by modern political ideas. The same was true of the Philippines, where the Sadkalist movement briefly brought thousands of peasants into open revolt against the existing authorities. Elsewhere in Southeast Asia, however, revolts could still take place which were of an essentially traditional character. Traditional appeals played a part in the Indonesian Communist uprisings of the late twenties, but the leaders fomented revolt with an ill-defined triumph of Communism in mind. In considerable contrast, the Saya San rising in Burma, despite its having been directed against the British colonial administration, seems to have been almost entirely traditional in both its aims and its methods. Cambodia passed through the twenties and thirties with only the slightest suggestion of opposition to French rule, while Malaya had yet to be awakened to the pressing problems of its divided society. The one Southeast Asian country which did not experience colonial rule, Thailand, experienced revolution in the form of a palace coup in 1932. Here the form of revolt was traditional, but the aims of its leaders were modern as they sought to end the absolute power of the king.

Retrospect permits the realization of how much potentiality for revolt was developed in the period before the Second World War. These were the facts which went largely unrecognized by the colonial governments in Southeast Asia. A Frenchman in the colonial administration in the late 1930s would have found it difficult, if not impossible, to believe that within less than twenty years there would no longer be a French Indochina. A British administrator would, in all probability, have found it difficult to conceive of an independent Malaya in which the potent threat of communalism was the chief concern. And a Dutch official, secure in his knowledge that the most important of those Indonesians who had challenged colonial rule were exiled in West New Guinea, could not have accepted that future generations of his countrymen would lose their hold over a vast eastern empire. The sudden change in the position of the colonial powers owed much to the Second World War and to the Japanese occupation. The way in which the various Southeast Asian countries responded to that climactic period was largely determined by the decades leading up to the war, in which programmatic appeals to revolt increasingly replaced the appeals cast in a traditional form.

In attempting even a brief survey of the colonial revolts which occurred in the twentieth century before the outbreak of the Second World War one faces considerable difficulty because of the uneven nature of the materials which are available for analysis. The Communist uprisings in Indonesia have benefited from a very considerable amount of analysis. The occurrences associated with the Nghe-An Soviets in Viet-Nam, by contrast, have still to be treated in detail. This disparity in the availability of material is so great that one of the most useful approaches to the period may lie in a discussion of the factors which led to particular revolts, rather than in a detailed account of the individual instances of revolt. Such an approach not only sets each revolt in some historical perspective. It also provides a point of departure for some consideration of those countries in which revolts did not occur.

The Growth of Modern Resistance in Viet-Nam

The period from the beginning of the present century to the outbreak of the First World War was critical for those in Viet-Nam who sought a sudden end to colonial status. Vietnamese of this persuasion had already separated themselves from those of their countrymen who were ready to accept the technical and educational benefits of French rule in return for political disenfranchisement.

The most notable of those who wanted revolutionary change was Phan Boi Chau, a man whose training had been in the Confucian classics, but whose political sympathies had been aroused by the reform ideas of such Chinese leaders as Liang Ch'i-chao. At first ready to believe in the virtues of constitutional advance, Phan Boi Chau and his associates came to accept that revolutionary change was the only way in which they could achieve their aims. The extent of their miscalculations as to the popular support which they would be able to excite in any attack upon the French administration was revealed in 1908. Attempting to capitalize upon peasant discontent in Central Viet-Nam in order to weaken French control, Phan Boi Chau and his supporters found that wider support for their aims of opposing the French could not be obtained. Moreover, the French colonial administration was able to demonstrate how effective its security forces could be in dealing with an ill-prepared opponent. Facing execution, exile or imprisonment, Vietnamese revolutionaries had to leave the political field to those who were prepared to accept French dominance.

The failure of those associated with Phan Boi Chau came at a time when there was ever-increasing political ferment in China. With the overthrow of the Chinese Empire in 1911 the appeal of revolution became even stronger in Viet-Nam. The Chinese experience after the revolution was to bring the formation of a Vietnamese political party based on the Kuomintang, and to provide the most famous Vietnamese politician of the century, Ho Chi Minh, with an introduction to the difficulties and importance of political organization in the pursuit of power. But whatever recognition there was of the significance of developments in China in the early years of the Chinese Republic, the application of its revolutionary ideas had to wait until after the conclusion of the First World War. This war brought the forced contact of many tens of thousands of Vietnamese with the West as they served in labour battalions in France and was important in increasing the degree of political awareness throughout Viet-Nam. The war also saw the emergence of the world's first Communist regime, and the significance of this event and its influence on Ho Chi Minh cannot be stated too highly.

In the decade which followed upon the end of the First World War the lines which separated constitutionalist Vietnamese from revolutionary Vietnamese were drawn ever more sharply. At the same time, the division between those who saw their revolutionary aims as part of a wider world upheaval and those who sought national rather than international change was equally sharply delineated. As for the first division, the twenties were years in which Vietnamese constitutionalists believed that the French colonial government would accept the need for slow progress towards independence, only to find that there was always a point beyond which they could not go. The French colonialists were prepared to give Vietnamese the opportunity to participate in politics. They were not prepared to give Vietnamese the right to determine their own future. The alternative was revolution and before the end of the twenties Ho Chi Minh was involved in the preparation for revolution.

Countless words have been expended in the debate over Ho Chi Minh's true political affiliations. Was he a nationalist revolutionary who saw Communism as a technique? Was he a Communist who mercilessly exploited nationalist tendencies? Such questions have been asked as if there was any sensible answer which could be made to them. The issue has been made more complex by the romantic wish of many who have opposed the Viet-Nam War to see in Ho a revolutionary figure who combined the various characteristics of an idealized stereotype. The most rewarding approach, in seeking some short assessment of Ho's politics, is to recognize that the dichotomies between nationalist and Communist which are so often suggested in the questions asked about him, seem unlikely to be ones which he would have recognized himself. The man who was a founding member of the French Communist Party could scarcely have been other than a Communist. Nor would the man who led a large part of his country to victory over the French deserve to be called other than a nationalist.

The difficulty has always been to know which strain predominated in his thinking at any period. Analysis has been made more difficult by the internationalist strain in Ho's thought. In the twenties Ho was part of an active group of Communists who learnt the theory of revolution in Moscow. There is no doubt that part of the attraction of this theory for him arose from the intense, as he saw it, economic exploitation of the Vietnamese population by the French. When the time came for Ho to start working in Viet-Nam his appeals to the peasants were cast in terms of colonial economic oppression.

As Ho and his fellow Communists were preparing for an attack upon French colonial control of Viet-Nam, another group of Vietnamese who had also drawn their inspiration from abroad were considering the possibility of revolutionary change. These were the members of the Vietnamese Nationalist Party (Viet-Nam Quoc-Dan Dang) who based their organization on the Chinese Nationalists. The tension between the Communists and Nationalists in China was reflected in the relations between the same groups in Viet-Nam. But possibly of greater importance than the reservations which each of these groups displayed towards the other was the different approach which each brought to the problems of developing membership and establishing a political organization. It was in the field of organization, above all else, that the Communists showed themselves pre-eminently able to overcome the continuous harassment of the French security authorities. While the Nationalists sought membership among the urban population, particularly among those occupying relatively junior positions in the French civil and military administrations, the Communists turned their attention to the peasantry as well as to discontented workers.

The accuracy of the Communist assessment that the peasantry could successfully be organized for political action was shown in the contrast between the Yen-Bay mutiny promoted by the Nationalist Party and the Nghe-An Soviets which emerged under Communist guidance. The Nationalist Party leaders placed their faith in terrorist attacks and the expectation that it would be possible to shake French control through a revolt of the Vietnamese troops serving under French control. Their hopes for a widespread rising failed in 1930 when only one garrison, that at Yen-Bay, mutinied against its French officers. This mutiny was quickly repressed and the leaders of the Nationalist Party who were well known to the French security services were arrested, and in some cases executed. The intended revolt was a failure and showed the limitations of the Nationalist approach. The lack of a mass base prevented the Nationalist efforts from being more than an isolated reaction against colonial rule. The conditions which had pushed the Nationalist leaders to open revolt had doubtless brought a widely felt resentment against the French in most Vietnamese urban centres. But resentment was of little importance unless it was channelled into action through organization.

The Communist-led revolts which broke out in the last few months of 1930, most dramatically in September, were not merely rural based. Communist organizations had been at work amongst the Vietnamese factory workers in the provinces of Nghe-An and Ha-Tinh, as well as amongst the peasantry. The remarkable fact about the revolt which developed was how successful the Communist cadres had been in their activities. Without more detailed information than is at present available we cannot know the nature of the appeals made to the peasants. Although many of the cadres had trained in China and could no doubt see the relevance of their theoretical studies to the conditions of a poor peasant in provinces which were traditionally amongst the poorest in Viet-Nam, the appeal of theory alone could scarcely be the motivation for the peasants' actions. Appeals of a much more general sort must be presumed. It is even too simple to argue that resistance to the alien French provides the basic explanation. Dislike of the French seems much more likely to have been subsumed within a massive resentment of a system of life which, for the inhabitants of Nghe-An and Ha-Tinh in particular, had become almost intolerable. French-decreed taxes were collected by Vietnamese officials in the French employ who by their grasping techniques of administration came to be some of the chief targets of peasant vengeance.

The scale of the revolts was sufficient to disrupt the functioning of the colonial administration and it was in this situation of administrative vacuum that the Communist organizers were able to establish the Nghe-An Soviets. Briefly, before French retribution came, the Communist leaders were able to claim that they had achieved revolution. When retribution overtook the movement it was terrible in its thorough suppression of those who had attacked colonial rule. The use of modern weapons of war and the deployment of troops from French African colonies resulted in considerable death and savage brutality. The accounts of this repression and brutality have mainly been presented by left wing French journalists whose reportorial technique was to heap horror upon horror; but even when read with the greatest circumspection, these accounts leave a stark picture of the measures to which a colonial regime would resort when it feared for its survival and had suffered a severe blow to its pride.

The end to the troubles in the north of Viet-Nam which was achieved by early 1931 represented little more than a temporary respite. The Indochinese Communist Party, as

the Vietnamese Communists were then known, had suffered as a result of the French repression, but its clandestine organization permitted it to survive underground
in a manner which the Nationalist Party could not emu-
late. Troubles in the north were followed by troubles in
the south of Viet-Nam, and throughout the thirties the
weakened Communists never failed to seize every opportunity for developing their widespread, if scattered, organization.

French pride in their colonial achievements has led to
myth-making about the 1930's, with the myths asserting,
concurrently, that Indochina was largely at peace before
the onset of the Second World War and that even Trotsky-
ites were allowed to play a political role in Cochinchina.
The situation in Viet-Nam was far more complex than
these myths suggest. Viet-Nam, Cambodia and Laos, the
countries making up French Indochina, were indeed relatively untroubled after the collapse of the 1930 revolts. But
this calm did not represent stability and it was achieved
through a massive security effort which meant that many
thousands of Vietnamese were detained in French colonial
prisons. The calm was an enforced calm with the colonial
power maintaining a monopoly on force. It is true that for
a short period the Vietnamese of Cochinchina – the southern third of modern South Viet-Nam – had freer political
opportunities because of Cochinchina's special status as an
extension of France rather than being a protectorate as
was the case with the central and northern sections of the
country. As part of 'Overseas France' Cochinchina had to
permit its native Communists the right to participate in
politics. But not only did this participation cease at the
point where the Vietnamese could actually play any active
part in the determination of affairs; even more importantly the period which saw relative freedom of participation lasted only from 1933 to 1939. With the outbreak of
the Second World War Communism was again anathema
to the colonial authorities and repression once again

became the rule. In reaction revolt flared in Cochinchina in late 1940, but at this time to no avail. The real revolt was to come after the major peace had been signed in 1945.

The Vietnamese experience of the four decades up to the outbreak of the Second World War had brought no certainty as to how the future would be resolved. Nevertheless, certain aspects of the Vietnamese situation had been clarified, at least from the point of view of those who opposed the French. The determination of the colonial power to resist any real sharing of responsibility with the indigenous population cut the ground from under the feet of those who sought gradualist solutions. Not only that, the repressive measures were a great aid to the one organization which was capable, both through its theories and its organizational ability, of maintaining its existence. Communism was not peculiarly suitable to the Vietnamese population at large. But its appeal to many intellectuals did relate directly to their own experience. One does not have to accept the Marxist interpretations of Vietnamese history to recognize that there was an important amount of economic exploitation in Viet-Nam. The subordination of Viet-Nam to French economic interests was largely complete. This was for young Vietnamese a classic example of the imperialist state's treatment of a colony. It was Viet-Nam's fate, or less dramatically its historical experience, that Marxist ideals should have appealed to men who proved themselves to be the best organized and the best able to lead. When the thirties drew to a close there was no guarantee that these men would triumph and that others would fail. Later events determined that Ho and his lieutenants would lead the fight against the French and gain control over half the country. The nature of French government in Viet-Nam, however, had played its part, so that when the Second World War came to Viet-Nam it provided a slow-acting catalyst which brought into play the widely felt resentment of the Vietnamese population.

Indonesia – Mistakes and Aftermath

No less than the French in Viet-Nam the Dutch administration of the East Indies (Indonesia) ruled through the
thirties with the satisfied belief that its presence would last
forever. This belief was founded on a number of premises
which, for an administrator of the period, must have
seemed unassailable. Within Java itself the last great challenge to colonial authority had been the Java War. Since
then the tranquillity of the most highly populated and
highly prized of the Dutch-ruled islands had only once
been disturbed on any major scale. This was as a result of
the Communist uprisings of 1926 and 1927 which also
affected the west coast of Sumatra. These uprisings took
place with such poor organization that they were quickly
put down. If the risings themselves posed little threat,
Dutch reaction to them was firm and effective and led not
only to the temporary destruction of the Communist organization within Indonesia, but also in succeeding years
to the deportation into exile of all Indonesians whose
political inclinations were judged to be dangerous to continuing colonial rule.

The shock of the Communist uprisings did not come because the Dutch in the past had ruled without resistance.
The colonial expansion of the closing years of the nineteenth century and the early years of the twentieth had
been a period of sometimes fierce and in some areas extended fighting. Dutch control over northern Sumatra had
only come after prolonged fighting against the Achenese,
who joined religious conviction to their fierce natural
bravery. The extension of Dutch rule over the island of
Bali had been accompanied by considerable bloodshed.
But these encounters with Indonesian resistance had taken
place before the First World War. The Communist uprisings were seen by the Dutch as a new and dangerous
phenomenon in which international politics played a per-
vasive part. In the eyes of the Dutchmen who reported on
the risings these revolts were of a different character from
the series of peasant movements which had persisted

through the colonial history of Indonesia. The agents of an international conspiracy had brought disturbance to a peaceful colony.

Later research has shown how ill-judged were the comments of many of the colonial officials who reviewed the Communist uprisings in Indonesia shortly after the event. There was an important element of Communist involvement in the risings, but many other elements were present, and indeed predominated. The revolts owe their significance to the reflection which they gave of the inability of the Indonesian Communist Party in the 1920s to provide leadership of the sort which could mount a successful challenge to the Dutch; to the way in which Communist-sparked revolts could bring under their banner a mass of disparate groups whose discontent showed a wide level of disorientation; and to the manner in which these ill-conceived risings placed the lid upon any prospects for political advance until the Japanese invasion. The Dutch Ethical Policy, which had been enunciated in 1901, and which had condoned a slow political advance for Indonesia, was put aside following the Communist-led risings.

By the early twenties the pace of political development amongst Indonesians had begun to accelerate. The first significant Indonesian political organization, Sarekat Islam, had moved beyond its initial concern for the commercial advancement of the indigenous population to involvement in that population's political interests. The early adherents to Communism in Indonesia at first worked as a group within Sarekat Islam, but by 1923 the Communists were acting as a separate party, convinced that change in the position of Indonesians would have to come through revolution.

Despite this conviction, the party refrained from violence for some years. Such a policy was ordered by the Comintern and it was approved by a number of the most important Indonesian members. When the outbreaks of revolt finally did come action was taken against the wishes of the Comintern. The decision to revolt against the

Dutch was made by second echelon leaders, frustrated by their impotence in the face of the colonial government. The call to revolt was answered by disoriented members of a growing urban proletariat; by peasants who, peculiarly, were without the social cohesiveness of other regions of Java and were inclined to fervid religious belief; and, in the view of one of the most interesting of the analyses, by men in a changing and even improving economic situation who saw in revolt the opportunity to improve their position within society.

The preparation for the revolt must rank as one of the least successfully concealed in modern history. The Dutch security forces had penetrated the Indonesian Communist Party and had broken the party's secret code. Foreknowledge of this sort enabled the colonial government to limit the outbreak of revolt in most of the main towns of Java; and even in Batavia the damage which the revolutionaries caused was small. With disagreement at the top of the Communist Party and a lack of careful preparation designed to mobilize the population at large, the relative success of the men who incited revolt in two areas is of considerable interest. In a section of west Java, Bantam, the revolt was of a much more serious order than in the urban concentrations. While persuasive suggestions have now been made that it is proper to speak of the 1926–7 risings as having a nationalist character, the revolt in Bantam certainly has parallels, too, with the millenarian peasant revolts which have occurred throughout Southeast Asian history. Communists were involved, but the appeal which they made to the peasants of the Bantam region had little to do with Communist theory. Just as appeals for support by Communists in urban areas included promises of free taxi rides, so did the appeals in a highly devout region speak of a religious utopia. Taxes would disappear and an earthly paradise would replace the difficulties of everyday existence. The insistence of the official reports made by the Dutch on the revolt in Bantam that the resistance which was mounted was of a new sort can never totally surmount the apparent similarities which the events of 1926 had with other peasant movements.

On the west coast of Sumatra the eruption of a Communist-led revolt came later in 1926 than the outbreaks on Java, and lasted longer. It also was the most costly in lives lost. The revolt in this area of Indonesia could not be described in the same traditionalist terms which seem to apply so readily to Bantam. But the major explanation for the extent of the revolt appears to lie in a very present feeling of frustration with the existing situation. Increasingly during the twentieth century the western section of Sumatra had been drawn into association with a wider world. Economic developments had altered older social patterns and brought resentment amongst those who felt that their progress was blocked by men whose claim to superiority rested on tradition rather than achievement. In Sumatra, as in the other areas where revolt broke out, the Communists appear to have offered all things to all men in seeking support. It is some measure of the desire for change that was present in the region that so many should have responded to these promises.

The loss of Dutch lives in the risings was negligible – one killed in Java and one in Sumatra. The psychological damage of the revolts to Dutch preconceptions was enormous. Arrests and deportations followed hard on the heels of the cessation of the revolts. Thirteen thousand Indonesians were arrested, of whom more than four thousand were eventually sent into exile. But more important than these immediate results were the long-term effects of the revolts. Convinced of international involvement in the affair, the Dutch were not prepared to tolerate any political activity which smacked of revolution. Throughout the 1930s the men who dreamed of Indonesian independence, whether it was to be achieved under Communism or some other political system, risked and endured exile. The Communist-led risings had shown how little importance the theory of Communism had for Indonesia in the 1920s. But it had also shown that a desire for change was just below the surface of relative peace which the Dutch maintained.

## The Absence of Revolt – Malaya and Cambodia

As the amount of material concerned with developments in Southeast Asia grows, so does it become more and more difficult to propose generalizations about the nature of the region's history. The untroubled calm of Malaya between the two world wars may still be a generally correct image, but it may require increasing qualification in terms of the evidence which has just begun to emerge of notable, if passing, Malay discontent with colonial rule. Even where violent revolt was absent, as in Malaya, this does not eliminate the interest which is to be found in evidence of the existence of popular resistance to colonial rule. Revolt in Cambodia, once the nineteenth century had ended, did not again take the violent form of the 1880s – at least, until after the Second World War when the Viet-Minh operated in the country. Yet any detailed political history of Cambodia would have to pay particular attention to the strange manifestation of peasant dissatisfaction which took place in 1916. This was not a violent affair. Quite to the contrary, since the tens of thousands of peasants who made their way to Phnom Penh in January 1916 came to receive their king's promise that their grievances would be considered, not to attack the colonial government which had almost completely circumscribed the king's power.

But if there were instances of mass resistance to British rule in Malaya and of peasants' movements in Cambodia, the fact remains that in these two countries revolt of the sort which was to be found in Viet-Nam was lacking. For this fact an explanation must be provided. Some of the most important answers are to be found in the nature of the colonial rule which existed in both countries. In Cambodia the French preserved the position of the king, providing him with even greater symbolic importance than he had enjoyed in the two or three centuries before the loss of Cambodian independence. Not only was the Cambodian monarchy maintained, but so too were the positions of the traditional Cambodian officials. In temporal matters both the king and his officials had to defer to the French in all affairs of importance, but the very preservation of their titles was some guarantee that the social structure of the country should be little changed. Those who received education came from the class which traditionally held positions of importance within the state. The absence of widespread education for the rest of the population meant that there was little spread of modern political concepts. In short, the elite which existed under the French control of Cambodia was, by and large, an elite which was accustomed to status and privilege. If rare men amongst this elite felt discontent at their lack of independence, this was not the general feeling of their fellows. Opportunities for wealth and advancement were linked with loyalty to the French administration and there is no evidence to suggest that this was a price which the majority were unwilling to pay.

Many of the same comments may be made about Malaya. Possibly even more than was the case with the French in Cambodia, the British officials in Malaya were prepared to respect the traditions of the Malay ruling group. The courtly Malay sultans were admired as possessing the attributes of British gentlemen – even more gratifyingly because this was so surprising. The educational programmes which were introduced into Malaya before the Second World War were cast in social as well as utilitarian form. The Malay aristocrat was given the opportunity for higher education, not the peasant. By the twenties and thirties the communal difficulties which became so significant in the years after 1946 could be clearly discerned, but the assumption was widely present that some solution would be found for the presence of increasing numbers of Chinese in Malaya without departing from the political programmes which were in existence. Such an attitude was aided by the fact that while there was some Chinese discontent with Malay privilege, the chief matter of political interest for a Chinese living in Malaya was the increasingly bitter struggle which was taking place between Communists and Nationalists in China.

Although the seeds of Malaya's later difficulties were identifiable in the 1930's, one would abuse the judgement of hindsight by seeing them as having made their presence significantly apparent. Malaya before the Second World War was an extraordinarily compartmented society with little thought in any of the separate communities about independence from Britain. The position occupied by the Malay sultans had very distinct similarities with the position held by the king of Cambodia. Where the sultans had once ruled uncertainly, worried about the threat of usurpation and frequently concerned with their financial position, British rule over Malaya had brought the Malay royal families wealth and an assured position. The palaces of the sultans with their stables of expensive cars provided a testimony to the advantages which British rule could provide the aristocrats. And because that same British rule had not interfered with the relationship between the sultans and their peasant followers, there was little questioning on the part of the less prosperous members of society about the disadvantages of their position.

In both Malaya and Cambodia, moreover, if there were periods of reduced prosperity, particularly in Malaya because of the Great Depression, there was little desperate poverty. Chinese in Malaya suffered during the Depression since their employment had been in industries affected by the world slump, though even these people could find land to work as squatters. The Chinese, however, were the one group in Malaya which experienced real problems of social disorientation. It was from amongst the squatter communities which lost employment during the Depression and then suffered persecution under the Japanese that the Chinese guerrillas of the Emergency came.

By and large, however, the absence of any major revolt in Cambodia and Malaya may be attributed to the general cause of an absence of major problems of social disorientation – either through excessive poverty or through disruption of old patterns of society – and the preservation of traditional political relationships as the result of a particular type of colonial rule. Most significantly, when revolt did erupt in Malaya it was almost solely the work of those Chinese who did not feel that they had a place within the compartmented plural society which was the mark of Malaya between the wars and continued after 1946. In Cambodia, equally significantly, the most serious armed challenge, as opposed to political challenge, to French control after the Second World War was mounted by alien Vietnamese as part of the Viet-Minh.

With the Southeast Asian region so troubled by political revolt in the period after the Second World War there has been a natural tendency on the part of many observers to stress the disruptive force of the European colonial presence in earlier years. Nationalist-minded Southeast Asian historians have frequently made this point as they seek to provide a new historiography in place of the accounts of their countries' past which have so often been provided by the same men who ruled over them in colonial times. There is, perhaps, some danger that an account of Southeast Asia which stresses the disruption of the colonial period will eclipse another quite notable feature of pre-independence history: the way in which colonial governments froze many of the difficulties and problems which had troubled Southeast Asia before the arrival of the European. Conflict between majorities and minorities, and between those who lived on the lowland plains and those of the upper regions, did not disappear during the period of colonial rule; but the conflict and tension were frequently rendered less acute. Nevertheless, when qualifications of this sort have been made, one must still take due account of the way in which colonial governments brought change to Southeast Asia; and sometimes with that change frustration and disorientation for the societies which they governed.

The slow introduction of modern education and the limited exposure of the most talented Southeast Asians to training in the metropolitan centres of Europe might be regarded, without exaggeration, as the setting of a time-bomb beneath the structure of colonial governments. Less altruistic measures adopted by colonial governments produced more easily identifiable reactions to colonial rule. Vietnamese revolutionaries, whatever their political persuasion, were convinced of the economic evils of French rule. Indonesian nationalists were aware of the disparity between the lot of their followers and the lives led by the people of Holland. The economic hardships which so frequently faced the peasants of Lower Burma are part of the explanation for the endemic discontent which was present in that region; and for such a dramatic outburst of resentment as occurred in the Saya San rebellion in which upwards of ten thousand Burmans were killed over a period of one year.

Change cannot come both rapidly and without any difficulty. The mistakes of the colonial governments were many and their failure to appreciate sufficiently the link between rapid change and discontent and disorientation in a society was one of their most notable faults. The relationship has not always been one which is appreciated by independent Southeast Asian governments. In seeking to trace and understand some of the factors which lie behind the particularly troubled history of Southeast Asia in the post-Second World War period, the extent to which Southeast Asian societies were affected by rapid changes over a wide range of their social, economic and political life in the twenties and thirties is singularly important. New political philosophies made their presence felt. New educational opportunities emphasized the contrast between the old and new orders. New economic demands brought the prospect of modernization at the cost of the destruction of old economic systems and the traditional values within society.

The impact of the Second World War on Southeast Asia

was of such a magnitude and importance that there is some danger of attributing to the wartime years almost all of the changes in attitude and capacity amongst the people of the region who engaged in revolt against colonial governments immediately after the war. It is difficult to overestimate the importance of the years between 1939 and 1945 for the subsequent development of Southeast Asia. Equally, it would be wrong to discount too easily the significance of the decades which had gone before. In the first four decades of the present century the changes which took place in Southeast Asia did not remove the importance of traditional beliefs and attitudes. Increasingly, however, those traditional aspects of life had to be reconciled with modernist concepts. Among the elite who were at the head of movements for political change were men who increasingly saw the future in terms of a programme. The nature and aims of the programme varied from group to group and country to country. In each instance the experience of the rapid change which had taken place since the beginning of the century had shaped the thinking of men who saw the future as requiring revolt against the established government as the only way to bring the new status which they craved for their countrymen.

# Chapter 5

# The Second World War

The widespread acceptance that the Second World War was a climactic event in the history of Southeast Asia may provide one of the explanations for the insufficient study which has been given to the period. Anyone with an interest in the area knows that it was during the years between 1942 and 1945 that some of the most important Southeast Asian nationalist groups were forged into active and viable forces. But the general image which attaches to the period seems blurred with the drama of the white man's temporary withdrawal and distorted by preconceptions about the role of the Japanese which date from the time of the war itself. Only recently has deeper study begun to probe the superficial outline in order to discover the reality which lies beneath. Such a task is a major one and this present short chapter cannot approach the issues and problems of the period in other than a brief fashion. What it does offer is some suggestion of the emphases which might be placed on the often confusing history of the period.

The Second World War and the Japanese occupation of Southeast Asia signalled the end of European colonial domination of the region. With the exception of the French administrators in Indochina, the Japanese advance brought the immediate overt humiliation of the colonial rulers: the vision of military defeat of Europeans by Asians; the complete reversal of roles in which Europeans became the prisoners and labourers of Asian overlords. Only in the states which made up French Indochina was this humiliation staved off for a time. The decision which Governor-General Decoux took not to resist the Japanese occupation of Indochina, in return for the right to maintain a French-run administration, was never the 'victory' which Decoux proclaimed it to be. For a time, however, the true relationship between the French colonial authorities and the Japanese was disguised until, in the closing months of the war, even the French tasted the bitterness of imprisonment at the hands of Asians.

The contrasts which the period of Japanese occupation brought forth cannot be stressed too greatly. One Chinese author writing of events in the Malayan area has spoken of 'the world turned upside down', and in immediate terms it is difficult to think of a better metaphor. When the Second World War began the leaders of the future Indonesian Revolution were, for the most part, political exiles languishing in the jungle internment camps of New Guinea. Ho Chi Minh and his followers maintained a tenuous existence on the northern borders of Viet-Nam, dependent on Chinese assistance and as distant as ever from the power which they sought over their homeland. Neither Malaya nor Cambodia had experienced any significant anti-colonial unrest and Laos slumbered in familiar forgotten tranquillity. In Burma nationalist activity was well established before the war began, but there was little indication that it would soon bring the withdrawal of the British. Only in the Philippines, by contrast, was progress towards independence already well established. What the war brought both in this country and in Malaya was the formation of important guerrilla groups led by Communists whose wartime anti-Japanese activity was to be transformed into anti-government endeavour after peace had come to the region.

The constant need to recognize the diverse as well as the common aspects of Southeast Asia emerges strongly in discussion of the effects of the Second World War. For this reason only a country by country survey, however brief, can set the scene for the surge of activity in which armed revolts were accompanied by national revolutions after 1945. Nevertheless, some very general indication must be given of the way in which reassessments are being made of the traditional picture of the Japanese occupation of Southeast Asia. Because of the tone and character of Japanese propaganda during the Second World War it is easy to forget that the Japanese were themselves regarded as colonizers by the populations of the various Southeast Asian countries. Slogans which stressed the common interests of 'Asians' had an attraction at first for nationalists; but this attraction was quickly dissipated when, to distort George Orwell's classic phrase, it was found that some Asians were more equal than others. The aim of the Japanese occupying forces to rule without opposition brooked no challenge and the memory of the *kempeitai*, the Japanese military police, which has survived in various of the occupied countries, reflects the role played by this group, with its heavy reliance on intimidation and physical violence.

Yet while older nationalist figures resented the manner in which one external ruler was replaced by another there is no doubt that the propaganda which the Japanese occupying forces disseminated had a profound effect on the thinking of younger persons, not least in Indonesia. And in Burma, in a way not equalled anywhere else in Southeast Asia, the onset of the Japanese occupation provided an opportunity for a nationalist military group, the Burmese Independence Army, to play a role in the development of nationalist activity which assured it of political dominance both after the war and into the 1960's.

In short, the effect of the Japanese occupation in stimulating nationalist endeavour in Southeast Asia was of an infinitely more complex nature than has, perhaps, been generally recognized. Emphasis on the blows struck at white prestige will long remain as important entries on the balance sheet. As time passes, however, it seems likely that observers will look back less to the all too frequent instances of brutality and more to the varying political significance of the war years in which the Japanese role varied so greatly from country to country.

## The Countries of Indochina — Viet-nam, Cambodia and Laos

After one major clash between the advancing Japanese armies and the French troops based in Viet-Nam the Vichyite administration agreed to a *modus vivendi* in which the Japanese were allowed free use of the Indochinese territories in return for the right of the French to maintain their civil control. Initially this provided little opportunity for those Vietnamese nationalists, both Communist and non-Communist, who were in exile from their homeland along the southern borders of China. But as the war advanced the members of the group controlled by Ho Chi Minh revealed their superior capacities as political, and more slowly as military, organizers. The efforts of the Nationalist Chinese to support the non-Communist Vietnamese exiles were foiled by Ho and his lieutenants – both by guile and when necessary by selective force. So much was this the case that when the Japanese came to recognize that their dreams of hegemony over Asia were fading the one group which was in any position to lead a movement against French colonial power was solidly linked with Communist leadership.

As the tide of the war turned against them the Japanese decided to overthrow the French regime which had survived to this point in the three Indochinese states and to place power in the hands of the Vietnamese, Cambodians and Laotians. In Viet-Nam the Japanese choice for a symbolic leader of a 'free' Viet-Nam was Bao Dai, the already partially discredited Vietnamese emperor whose dynasty had come to power in 1802. Neither Bao Dai nor his ministers, however, was in a position to establish an administration which could challenge the alternative force which now emerged from the hills of northern Tonkin. The Viet-Minh (the shortened form of a name meaning the Vietnamese Independence League) had, according to Vo Nguyen Giap himself, no more than one thousand soldiers at the time of the Japanese *coup de force* in March 1945. But these men and the core of civilian administrators which Ho now promoted as the true leaders of the Vietnamese state were unchallenged by any other similarly equipped or determined group. To make this observation is not to deny that there were many Vietnamese who did not share Ho's aims or politics; but what seems undeniable is the fact that the leadership of the Viet-Minh was both efficient and, despite their adhesion to Communism, imbued with a nationalist commitment. Those who stood in the way of the Viet-Minh risked death just as would have been the case for Ho's cadres if their opponents had had more foresight and ability. Viet-Nam has seldom been a country lacking in political violence.

The success of the Viet-Minh at this stage of the Vietnamese revolution was uneven. Although the Viet-Minh forces in the north were able to implant themselves for a period in Hanoi the early occupation of Saigon by British forces was a blow against the Communist efforts in the south. It was, moreover, to be many years before the Viet-Minh was able to carry out its plans for political indoctrination in wide areas of the countryside, so that to speak of mass support at this stage would be misleading. Yet when all these qualifications are made it remains important to perceive the phenomenal progress which the revolutionaries had made. At the time of the Japanese coup the Viet-Minh forces were about one thousand men. Little more than six months later when the Japanese were defeated the forces at Viet-Minh command had only risen to a little more than five thousand. But more importantly when Ho proclaimed the independence of the Vietnamese republic in September 1945 he did so before an enthusiastic crowd of half a million gathered in Hanoi. The proclamation came after Ho's emissaries had persuaded Bao Dai to abdicate and at a time when many of the most able men in Viet-Nam, whatever doubts they had about the political orientation of the emerging government, had become convinced that effective opposition to the French meant association with the Viet-Minh.

The fundamental change in the Vietnamese situation

at this stage was the result of many threads of history suddenly knit together by the Second World War. There was nothing inevitable about any one of these developments, but after the political repression which had characterized French rule for most of the preceding fifty years the Japanese occupation and the Japanese defeat, combined with the humiliation which the French colonial government had undergone, left the way open to the one group in Viet-Nam which was ready and able to seize power.

By contrast the developments in Cambodia and Laos seem unexciting indeed. In both of these countries – the term being only dubiously applicable to Laos – the Japanese overthrow of the French administration led to the inauguration of new regimes. In each case, however, the new regimes retained their identification with the royal representative who had held the throne as a French pensioner before the *coup de force*.

This is not to say that the change was without significance. The slow emergence of King Norodom Sihanouk into an active political role in his country may be dated from this time despite the fact that it was not until some five or six years later that his involvement became firmly associated with the goal of ending French control of Cambodia as quickly as possible. And it was also in this brief period of Japanese-supported Cambodian independence from French control that Sihanouk's one real challenger for leadership of the country in the post-war period, Son Ngoc Thanh, came into real prominence. Nor, despite the eternally near comic opera nature of Laotian politics, was the period without considerable later significance for Laos because of the role played by the future Pathet Lao leader Prince Souphanouvong. In this latter case, Souphanouvong's early association with the Viet-Minh suggests that one of the most rewarding ways to understand the history of Laos from 1945 until the present time is through considering it in its traditional role as a border area or buffer state in contest between Viet-Nam and Thailand. Forces on the left came to support one section of Laotian opinion just as forces on the right came to support another, while yet others sought to pursue a neutralist policy, which had never previously been a policy open to the principalities of the region.

The great difference between the experiences of Viet-Nam on the one hand and Cambodia and Laos on the other was the fact that in the latter two the French were able, after the war, to establish their authority over most of the population. This was never the case in Viet-Nam.

## Burma

Only in Burma did the invading Japanese forces have the assistance of an organized army convinced of its nationalist character which fought against the colonial power. The Burmese Independence Army (BIA), headed by men who had been trained by the Japanese outside Burma before the Second World War began, advanced with the Japanese into Burma, driving the colonial administration into retreat. The military success of the BIA was not major, but the political importance of the military leaders involved was great. So long as the BIA existed – it was disbanded in 1942 – Burmese nationalists could point to the part played by their own troops in ridding the country of the colonial power. When the army was disbanded the military leaders did not disappear from the scene. They took posts in the new armed forces which the Japanese sponsored and finally turned against their new colonial masters when it became apparent that the Japanese would be unable to resist the return of the Allied forces.

The complicated internal politics of Burma in the war-time and immediately post-war period make summary difficult. The interests of those who had served with the BIA and those who had been associated with other nationalist movements were not always at one. The point of greatest interest is that here as in other countries of the Southeast Asian region the Japanese occupation marked a point of no return. Large numbers of Burmese had enjoyed the attractive experience of political and military power. The limits on that power were closely set by the Japanese, it is true. The experience was sufficient, however, to present the returning British administration with a clear indication of the need to heed the Burmese call for independence. Partly as an accompaniment to British desires to disengage from the Indian sub-continent, and partly as a reflection of the depth of feeling in Burma itself, the decision for withdrawal came relatively quickly and easily. That independence did not solve the ancient problem of an ethnically divided state has been abundantly demonstrated since 1948. In the perspective of the Second World War, however, the events in Burma were a striking affirmation of the way in which that period changed the face of Southeast Asia.

## Indonesia

Only in the Indonesian islands had colonial rule in the period before the Second World War approached the degree of political repression which had been such a mark of French control in Viet-Nam. The calm tenor of life in the Indies hid the fact that those Indonesians who showed any real commitment to nationalist endeavour were in exile, either, by their own choice, outside the Dutch colony or, at the will of the colonial rulers, within it. In this situation the arrival of the Japanese provided a complete transformation of the political and social assumptions which had been inherent in Dutch rule. Not only were nationalist exiles able to return to their homes and permitted to play an increasingly important political role. Coincidentally, the presence of the Japanese in Indonesia disseminated amongst younger Indonesians new ideas and new attitudes which had an almost incalculable effect in changing basic Indonesian attitudes or, more particularly Javanese attitudes, among the younger generation.

The men who were to participate in the leadership of the post-war Indonesian revolution, Sukarno and Hatta being the most notable, chose to co-operate with the Japanese during the wartime period. This co-operation was

F

later to bedevil the Dutch reaction to the Indonesian demands for independence. For the former colonial power it was all too easy to equate the Asian collaborator with the European quisling. For the course which Indonesian history followed in the post-war period the importance of co-operation lay in the way in which the wartime years emphasized the need to develop an organizational apparatus, one which could change fragmented political cliques into widely based movements.

Increasingly, students of the wartime period in Indonesia are laying stress on the extent to which the Japanese occupation brought changes among the youth of the country. Although it seems correct to argue that in general Japanese rule was resented by Indonesians, it is nonetheless apparent that for the younger generation in Java there was much in Japanese political philosophy that was attractive. This was not merely a case of youthful Indonesians being attracted by the anti-white preachings of the Japanese. Much more was involved. The Japanese stress on force and on demonstrative military behaviour presented great contrasts with traditional Javanese values. While not wholly accepted by younger Indonesians, these values played a part in accentuating the generational differences between the old and the young. The differences became sharper when many younger Indonesians came to feel that those who co-operated with the Japanese, pre-eminently men who had already reached a reasonably mature age, bore some responsibility for Japanese harshness and brutality in their administration.

Although the Japanese in Indonesia did not act, as they did in Indochina, to institute a 'free' indigenous government before the arrival of the Allied forces, they moved close to it. Before the end of the war Indonesians were meeting with Japanese approval to discuss independence, and the proclamation of that independence came only two days after the final Japanese surrender. Four years were then to pass before the Indonesian demand for independence was met by the Dutch in 1949. The war had ensured that the demand for independence would come and the Japanese occupation despite its contradictions played a large part in this. By giving administrative and military experience to substantial numbers of Indonesians the Japanese occupation provided a core of trained men who could assume vital roles when the armed clash came with the returning Dutch. The thirties had put a damper on any hopes for real Indonesian independence. Three years of Japanese occupation permitted the resurgence of nationalist activity and the development of an organized group whose aim of revolt against Dutch control now had the benefit of organization to match its enthusiasm.

## Malaya and Singapore

In occupying Malaya the Japanese made no promises of future independence and made no major effort to encourage the development of nationalist feeling. There was no group with nationalist aims in Malaya before the war comparable to those found in Viet-Nam or Indonesia. Even more importantly, the Japanese in Malaya were dealing with an ethnically divided population which included a large Chinese minority sympathetic to those who had fought and were fighting against the Japanese in China. While the Japanese gave special consideration to the Malays – placing them in positions which had the appearance if not the reality of power – they treated the Chinese with harshness which often became brutality.

There is no doubt that the period of the Japanese occupation played a part in developing a sense of national identity amongst Malays and in raising for the first time the possibility that in the future they would be able to think in other than colonial terms. British power could never be regarded as omnipotent after the swift defeat which the Japanese had administered. Yet when these points are noted, the effect on the Malays of Malaya was considerably less than that of the dramatic challenge which was mounted to British power by Malayan Chinese after the war had ended. The Emergency which began in 1948 was a direct flow-on from the activities of the Chinese Communist guerrillas who led the resistance against the Japanese during the war. Organized and led by Communists, the Chinese guerrillas in Malaya were the one significant resistance movement which operated against the Japanese. Because of this the Allied forces decided to aid them in their efforts and in 1943 a special military group was formed and infiltrated into Malaya to co-ordinate guerrilla activity. This group, Force 136, played an extremely important part in training and equipping the Chinese guerrillas, who had adopted as their name the Malayan People's Anti-Japanese Army.

With the end of the war the returning British authorities saw the danger of a Communist-led para-military group retaining its identity and its arms, and efforts were made to disband and disarm the Chinese guerrillas. These efforts were never entirely successful and after 1948, until when Communist activity had been open in character, the former members of the Malayan People's Anti-Japanese Army came to form the nucleus of the guerrilla challenge to the British colonial government in Malaya. The period which followed is now known as the Emergency.

## The Philippines

In the Philippines also the period of the Second World War saw the emergence of a Communist-led guerrilla group which played an important part in providing armed resistance to the Japanese. This group, the Hukbalahap* (usually shortened to Huks) had its roots in the peasant discontent which was common in large areas of the Philippines, particularly in central and southern Luzon. During the wartime period the Huks gained an important reputation as the protectors of the people at a time when despite a general opposition to the occupation there were a significant number of Filipinos who were prepared to co-

* Hukbalahap is, itself, a short form of the Tagalog words meaning 'People's Army Against the Japanese'.

operate with the Japanese.

The fact that the Huks received a considerable amount of support from the peasants in the areas where they operated, and that they were Filipinos themselves, set them apart from the Chinese guerrillas who fought against the Japanese in Malaya. Their territorial base was, however, fairly circumscribed; and in making their calls for political change, as opposed to fighting against the Japanese, they confronted a solidly entrenched traditional governing group which had no interest in social transformation of the sort which the Huk leaders envisaged. The Huk's advantages, and their disadvantages, make their movement an object of particular interest in the post-war period. Their emergence into prominence must again be counted one of the important results of the Japanese era in Southeast Asia.

## Thailand

Alone amongst the countries of Southeast Asia, Thailand did not experience colonial rule. When, in order to avoid the disasters which they were certain would follow upon resistance, the Thai leaders agreed to permit the Japanese to enter their country and to use it as a base for operations against other regions, the Thai Government ensured that its own internal authority survived. It is not correct to see a parallel between events in the French Indochinese states and those in Thailand. In Viet-Nam the French retained their administrative control at the pleasure of the Japanese and that administrative control was colonial in nature. While the Thai Government could not disregard the interests of the Japanese, its members did not rule by virtue of the Japanese presence. The Japanese occupation did not present the opportunity for nationalist groups to organize for the future since, whatever judgement may be made about the policies which it pursued, the government of Thailand already had a national identity. Thailand thus emerged from the Second World War little affected by the Japanese occupation. Just as its lack of colonial experience made it unique, so did the nature of Thailand's contact with the Japanese again separate the country from those general features of the Second World War period which may be discerned in the rest of Southeast Asia.

In the years immediately after the Japanese surrender the gloomiest forebodings of those who feared change seemed justified. In the case of Burma an adjustment between the colonial power and the nationalists came quickly. But this was not the case in Indonesia nor in Viet-Nam. In both the Philippines and Malaya attacks were mounted against the existing government by Communist-led organizations which for a brief period seemed to pose a very real threat to the continued stable existence of the state. Viewed with the perspective provided by the lapse of twenty years, it might very well be argued that the condition of Southeast Asia gave supporters of established regimes much more cause for concern then than it does today. Certainly the spectre of Communism was very much abroad when an observer's gaze focused on developments in Viet-Nam, Malaya and the Philippines.

Yet the cataclysms which were so readily perceived at that time did not come to pass. Viet-Nam came to be partially controlled by a Communist administration. But that bald observation hides the distinctive history of a country in which to attempt to separate the concept of nationalism from Communism carries with it the gravest risk of distortion. In Malaya the challenge to established authority which took place during the Emergency was defeated. The Huks in the Philippines could not rally sufficient support to achieve their aims.

As one moves closer to the present, the difficulty of summarizing events in Southeast Asia grows greater. Either one faces a mass of undigested information, as is so often the case in relation to developments in Viet-Nam; or for any of a number of reasons an episode which appears fascinating in itself has not received the detailed study which allows an observer to do much more than identify some of the most obvious features – the regional revolt of the outer regions of Indonesia against the central authority or the situation which developed in Cambodia in 1970 are, perhaps, examples of this. In describing and discussing revolt in Southeast Asia in the period since the Second World War it becomes essential to be selective. The experience of the Viet-Nam War has demonstrated the dangers of assuming that developments in one Southeast Asian country are readily transferable to another. Just because the Chinese guerrillas were defeated in Malaya and the Huks' challenge was blunted in the Philippines, it has too often been assumed that the techniques which were used in these situations could be readily applied elsewhere. For this reason, amongst many others, anyone who seeks to understand the problem of revolt in Southeast Asia must give particular attention to the Emergency and the Huk Rising – the revolts which failed – and to the Viet-Minh challenge to French authority – the revolt which half succeeded.

# Chapter 6

## Malaya and the Philippines: Two Revolts that Failed

The end of the Second World War brought peace to Malaya and the return of a British-controlled administration. However, even in this, one of the most settled of the Southeast Asian colonial possessions during the 1930's, the war years had ensured that there could be no simple return to previous arrangements of government. The British authorities faced a mass of problems, but in essence these all fell under one major heading: the need to devise some form of government which took account of the diverse racial composition of the Malayan population.

The Malays of Malaya, representing something less than fifty per cent of the population in the immediate post-war period, had been protected throughout British colonial times and were officially regarded as the sole 'people of the country' – the only persons who deserved to have special rights to land and preferment in government employment. The Chinese, in very considerable contrast, had been regarded through most of the period leading up to the Second World War as temporary residents, essential to the economic well-being of the country but not requiring any substantial political rights. Seeking some new compromise after the war, initial British efforts to institute a Malayan Union which would have given some power to the Chinese population at the expense of the Malays failed, and the Federation of Malaya which was established in 1948 preserved essential Malay rights.

In these difficult circumstances, with the colonial power endeavouring to find a satisfactory and peaceful solution to Malaya's ethnic-dominated politics, the Malayan Communist Party (MCP) came to play an increasingly active part. The British were quite successful in their efforts to disband the Chinese guerrilla forces which had fought against the Japanese during the war, and in collecting weapons which had been issued to these guerrillas. But the organizational basis which the war had provided for the guerrillas never completely disintegrated. In the hectic years of 1946 and 1947 the Malayan Communist Party, which was almost totally Chinese in composition, maintained pressure upon the colonial administration through open techniques – strikes, the intimidation of non-Communist workers and occasional violence against government offices in rural areas. To some extent the activities of the Communists were a reflection of the approaching crisis in the Chinese Civil War. Heartened by the Chinese Communist Army's successes against the Nationalist forces, the members of the MCP were emboldened to act vigorously against those Chinese in Malaya who still supported the Kuomintang. At the same time, the actions taken by the MCP in Malaya were an attempt to capitalize upon the unsettled conditions in the country and the uncertain status of the Chinese community, as a whole, in Malaya. Of capital importance to the MCP's efforts, once open insurrection began, was the large Chinese squatter community which provided a source of recruits, intelligence and supplies. Just as importantly, the fact that Communist strategy came to depend so heavily on this squatter group provided the government forces with one of their most important means to combat the open challenge which faced them from 1948.

By the end of the war there were some half million Chinese squatters in Malaya. The bulk of these people had not been born in Malaya. They were without significant wealth and without any identification with the colonial government. Their great significance for the Malayan Emergency lay in the fact that it was essentially a Chinese rebellion against the existing government in which the Malays, the people of the country, played no part. When the Communists decided in 1948 that they would follow a programme of armed insurgency in place of the earlier attempts to advance their position through strikes and intimidation it was upon the squatters that their strategy depended. Although their numbers never rose above eight thousand men, the guerrilla units could look to the squatters for a high degree of co-operation, either willing or coerced, as they struck from their jungle bases against isolated plantations, government outposts and the Malayan transport system.

Whether the Communist insurgency in Malaya developed as the result of a planned programme of revolt for the Asian region following the Calcutta Youth Conference of February 1948, has been a matter for academic debate. Whatever the truth may be, the insurgency began in June 1948 when guerrillas struck against rubber planters in the state of Perak. From this time onward, until 1954, the insurgents followed a policy directed principally against European planters in isolated plantations, and the representatives, whatever their ethnic origin, of the Malayan Government. These attacks, which frequently led to the death of men on both sides, represented the first stage in the Communists' overall strategy. The insurgents were aware that Malaya's economy was basically founded upon the large mining and plantation ventures scattered throughout the country. Taking the already established Chinese model of revolution as the basis for their efforts, the insurgents envisaged two further stages to follow the economic collapse which they foresaw following their first attacks. Stage two was to come with the establishment of areas under insurgent control; these would be the familiar 'liberated zones' of Communist revolutionary theory. Stage three was to be achieved when the insurgents as the core of a liberation army would join with the population in a general uprising to take control of Malaya.

The plan was grandiose and unrealistic. But although the insurgents never passed beyond the first phase of their aims, their efforts were sufficient to tie down large numbers of British and Commonwealth troops for many years before the Emergency could be considered under adequate control.* The insurgents inflicted significant casualties on the security forces and civilians, so that during 1951 the insurgents were credited with causing seven deaths per day. And they were able to damage, even if they failed signally to achieve their aim of disrupting, the Malayan economy. In a world which has witnessed the costs of Viet-Nam, in terms of both lives and expenditure, the numbers involved in the Emergency operations, on both sides, and the casualties suffered seem small. This particular perspective should not diminish the extent to which the Emergency represented a real challenge to established authority in Malaya, nor the way in which, particularly in 1950 and 1951, it seemed difficult to predict any quick end to the insurgency.

As a Chinese insurgency in a country where the Chinese were neither a majority nor had any tradition of support from the Malays, the Malayan Emergency may very well be described as a 'special situation'. Such a term can be used for almost any insurgency when one considers the extent to which each is the product of the particular features of the country and society in which it took place. Nevertheless, the term may have special relevance to the Emergency period. This seems so when it is realized that neither in the Philippines nor in Viet-Nam, the other countries in which Communist-led revolts broke out after the end of the Second World War, was the insurgent group distinguishable from the rest of the population on an ethnic basis. As a minority group within Malaya, and within their own ethnic minority, the Communist insurgents in the Emergency period faced immensely difficult problems in their efforts to move beyond sporadic attack to any general offensive.

* The Emergency was proclaimed on 17 June 1948 for the states of Johore and Perak, and extended to the whole of the Federation of Malaya the following day. Most writers agree with the estimation that the major problems of the Emergency had been overcome by 1954. Nevertheless, the Emergency was not finally declared ended until 31 July 1960.

For the first two or three years of the Emergency period (1948–51) the Malayan Government was faced with the need both to counter insurgent attacks and to formulate a programme which would permit the security forces to move on to the initiative. Resettlement of the squatter communities which could provide so much assistance to the Chinese guerrillas became a top priority in this situation. The sudden eruption of the Emergency showed just how inadequate was the colonial government's knowledge of the squatters. The size of the squatter population was not known with any accuracy and the investigation which now began revealed the quite extraordinary extent to which the squatters lived without any real contact with the administration. It was apparent that unless these squatters were brought under normal administrative control only the insurgents could benefit. As the first serious efforts were made to resettle or regroup squatters to ensure government control, an overall strategic plan (known as the Briggs Plan after the then British High Commissioner in Malaya) was set forth in 1950. The Briggs Plan's objectives were lucidly enunciated in four principal aims:

1. To dominate the populated areas and to build up a feeling of complete security which would in time result in a steady and increasing flow of information coming from all sources.
2. To break the Communist organizations within the populated areas.
3. To isolate the bandits from their food and supply organizations in the populated areas.
4. To destroy the bandits by forcing them to attack the security forces on their own ground.

In order to make this plan a success the government had to be able to muster sufficient military forces to carry on operations against the insurgents over protracted periods and away from settled areas. At the same time it had to be sure that there were sufficient police forces which could combine the tasks of protecting those in the civilian population who were not in sympathy with the insurgents and those who either through sympathy or fear were prepared to co-operate with them. Such demands meant that both military operations against the insurgents and the resettlement programme had to begin slowly. In Johore state, for instance, which was one of the most important in terms both of insurgent activity and the number of squatters who had to be regrouped or resettled, the resettlement programme was not completed until May 1951, despite the fact that military operations were given priority in this state and the number of squatters involved was approximately sixty-six thousand.

As squatters were brought under government control their security became the responsibility of the police and the home guard. The importance of the latter may not have been great, except in terms of building civilian morale by having as many persons as possible associated with the government effort. The importance of the police, in contrast, cannot be overestimated. The ranks of the police force were chiefly filled by Malays who served with devotion during the Emergency. The most senior officers were British. But special mention should be made of the able Chinese police officers whose knowledge of the Chinese community was invaluable in the collection and evaluation of police intelligence. With protection assured, the ideal provided for the government to ensure that the resettled communities were given essential services, including schools and a medical clinic, in the 'new villages' as the resettlement areas were called. This ideal was generally attained, but it would be misleading not to record the many occasions, particularly at the beginning of the resettlement scheme, when this was not the case. Squatters were resettled on land which could not provide them with adequate opportunities to engage in agriculture. Essential services, and even housing, were on occasion lacking. And even more dramatically, there were instances when government protection of the new villages could not prevent the insurgents from striking against those who had been resettled.

Before the end of the Emergency over half a million squatters were either resettled or regrouped. As the opportunities for the insurgents to draw upon these formerly isolated communities for recruits and supplies dwindled so did the main force security units devote an increasingly large amount of their time to operations deep in the jungles of Malaya where the insurgents maintained their base camps in an effort to avoid government patrols. When it is remembered that the guerrillas never numbered more than eight thousand men, the high cost of anti-guerrilla operations is shown in the fact that there was a total of three hundred thousand government personnel engaged against them. There were some forty thousand regular British and Commonwealth troops, including some of the British Army's most highly regarded regiments. The Malayan police forces totalled some seventy thousand and there were some two hundred thousand home guards whose duties were mainly as static guards. The contrast between the numbers involved on each side during the Malayan Emergency has been one of the factors leading to the often quoted assertion that the suppression of a guerrilla insurgency requires a ratio of ten to twelve government troops to one guerrilla.*

The achievement of military success in Malaya was vitally linked to the way in which an efficient resettlement scheme was used to isolate the one section of the Malayan population whose assistance was vital to the military operations of the insurgents. This isolation of the squatters from the insurgents thus had a strong negative aspect to it. Whether the Malayan Emergency involved the government going beyond negative measures and the introduction of overwhelming force to achieve its military ends is a matter over which there is some opportunity for discussion. The official accounts of the Malayan Emergency, and

* Such a numerical superiority, it may be noted, was achieved without the participation of the home guard units.

above all the pronouncements made by General Sir Gerald Templer when he was High Commissioner in Malaya, stressed that more was involved in the government's approach to the guerrilla challenge than military operations. In a phrase which has now become banal through overuse, the Malayan Government spoke of its efforts to win 'the hearts and minds of the people'. The concept involved was sound: that it was impossible to achieve any lasting resolution of the problems of Malaya unless the Chinese community was brought to play a part in Malayan society as a whole. Sir Gerald Templer's own techniques in seeking to convince the resettled communities that there was no alternative to becoming part of the wider community were the subject of controversy in the early fifties. Then, refusal to give information to the government or more seriously in the eyes of the administration, the provision of supplies to the insurgents led to the punishment of entire communities through the application of punitive curfews.

The arguments in favour of such techniques were, fundamentally, that harsh times demanded harsh measures. But not all of the efforts to win over the uncommitted resettled squatters were of this sort. It was of the greatest importance that despite the propaganda mounted by the insurgents the government was able to show that progress was being made towards the achievement of Malayan independence. Moreover, a Chinese party, the Malayan Chinese Association (MCA) could be seen to be associated with the movement towards independence. It may very well be that much of the propaganda which the MCA directed at the squatters was too sophisticated for people who had previously had no contact with concepts of democratic government. Nevertheless, it would be wrong to discount the importance of the MCA as an alternative focus of appeal. The government ensured that facilities were extended to the MCA to campaign in the new villages. But quite apart from the politically oriented efforts of the MCA the government was constantly at work seeking to bring home to the resettled squatters the contrast beween the opportunities which a peaceful multi-racial Malaya offered them and the dubious prospects of life under a Communist-controlled state. In this effort the government was able to make use of those guerrillas who had surrendered and who were ready to speak against their former comrades in arms. These surrendered enemy personnel were not the least remarkable feature of the Malayan Emergency. Having once surrendered, many of them appear to have undergone a genuine change of heart. From this point on they supplied intelligence to the administration and in many cases were ready to address resettled squatters stressing the harsh life led by the guerrillas.

There need be no doubt that the successful conclusion of the Malayan Emergency represented a brilliant military operation. Particularly under Templer's direction, there was a close and successful intermeshing of all phases of government activity against the insurgents. Military, police and civil efforts were integrated and operated efficiently. Ironically, given the claims which the insurgents made to be fighting against British imperialism, this efficiency owed much to the fact that ultimate power in Malaya still lay in British hands. This is not merely to suggest that British personnel were more efficient than Malayan personnel. Rather the importance of continuing British control lay in the fact that, in the long run, the British could shoulder the opprobrium which the sometimes harsh decisions taken by the government produced. The Malayan official, be he Malay, Chinese or Indian, could carry out a resettlement order which might provoke the resentment of his countrymen secure in the knowledge that ultimate responsibility for the decision lay elsewhere.

As the rate of resettlement increased, so were the British and government troops able to bring greater pressure to bear upon the insurgents. The government and military intelligence services had not been completely without significant information on the leaders of the insurgency from the very beginning. As the years went by the volume of information on the guerrillas increased to the point where it was possible for the government security forces to make direct appeals to individual insurgents to surrender. Although there were some notable setbacks to government progress, not least when the insurgents succeeded in subverting groups of Malayan aborigines to their assistance, once the early years of the Emergency had passed there was little doubt of the outcome of the battle. The Chinese guerrilla groups were never completely eliminated and the jungles of the Thai-Malayan border still shelter the rump of the guerrilla units who had fought during the Emergency and their leader Chin Peng. There need, however, be no doubt who won in this insurgency.

There are many ways of looking at the Malayan Emergency. It has, far too often, been seen as a classic example of the way to defeat an internal insurrection mounted against an established administration. In particular the programme of resettlement has been regarded as a fundamental guide to the problems of pacification in Viet-Nam. In a more restricted perspective, the Emergency has been presented as the successful containment of armed challenge to the existence of a peaceful Malayan state. Both of these manners of considering the Emergency require considerable qualification.

The success of the military operation against the insurgents was an essential for the emergence of an independent Malaya in 1957. At a rather deeper level, however, one may still ask if the lessons of the Emergency awoke the dominant Malayan politicians to the dangers of perpetuating an arrangement in which political power is concentrated in the hands of one racial group while another, almost of the same size, is left with perceptibly less access to that power. The initial success of the MCP in attracting support reflected the way in which a substantial number of Chinese living in Malaya felt no identification whatsoever with the existing governmental and administrative system. Many were convinced of the virtues of Communism, but it would be wrong to attribute a deep belief in

97

that political theory to all of the insurgents. What does appear to have been a common belief, at least initially, was that membership of the guerrilla bands would give them the opportunity to be associated with an organization which was committed to improving their lot and which offered them an alternative to the alienated state in which they had previously found themselves. For a former squatter, a low paid urban worker or a city clerk bewildered by the post-war world, it was not difficult to accept that the British-controlled government of Malaya was the cause of their unsatisfactory position. The indoctrination and rigorous discipline which was imposed on those who joined the guerrillas was far from unwelcome to men who had felt neglected by authority and who had lacked any firm purpose in their daily lives. It is a telling comment on the squatter communities from which many of the insurgent recruits were drawn that these, in contrast to long-established Chinese communities in Malaya, were lacking in social cohesiveness. In agricultural activities there was none of the traditional Chinese concern to make careful use of the soil.

Only an alarmist would suggest that, having defeated the Communist challenge during the Emergency, the Malayan Government and its Malaysian successor have followed policies which are likely to lead to another insurgent challenge of the same proportions. It would be equally mistaken for an observer of Malayan affairs to fail to take account of the fact that the military success of the Emergency has not led to any reassessment of the overall political balance of the country. The Chinese guerrillas who struck in 1948 acted because they felt themselves denied the opportunities which the Malayan Government offered to its population. Today, with no real threat of armed insurgency, there is still reason to argue that the problem of the Chinese within the Malaysian state has not been satisfactorily resolved. Almost equal in numbers to the Malays in West Malaysia (Malaya), the Chinese must continue to live within a compromise arrived at in the middle fifties which gave paramount political power to the Malays and opportunities for commercial success to the Chinese. In short, the Emergency demonstrated the way in which it was possible to resolve a politico-military problem without necessarily coming to terms with a deeper and interconnected problem in Malayan society. Or, to rephrase the conclusion, the successful end to the Emergency may be termed the elimination of the extreme aspect of the problems affecting Malaya's plural society. One looks with little success for efforts to resolve the problems which have not yet become extreme.

Yet if these qualifications are noted, should due attention not be given to the way in which the experience gained in Malaya provides a guide to combating insurgency elsewhere? Earlier Malaya was termed a 'special situation', and the factors involved in applying such a term to the Malayan Emergency suggest that severe qualification is necessary before any assumption is made that techniques used there will be successful in other insurgency situations. There are, of course, some military similarities between problems which were faced in Malaya and problems faced later in Viet-Nam. In both instances the established government was faced with the necessity of protecting a rural population which either willingly or otherwise was prepared to help the insurgents. From the point of view of the aims of those waging their insurgency against the established government also, both Malaya and Viet-Nam have sustained liberation wars. But even before the massive escalation of the war in Viet-Nam since 1965 the similarities between the two situations seem to have been far outweighed by the differences.

In Malaya an ethnically separate group mounted an insurgency against an established government in which the prospects for political power lay in the hands of another ethnic group. The Emergency was a Chinese insurgency in which the Malays gave practically no support to the insurgents. The revolt against the British Government in Malaya took place at a time when independence had still not been achieved, but when the colonial authorities were able to demonstrate that they had a clear intention of handing powers of government over to an independent Malayan administration. None of these circumstances had any clear parallel with Viet-Nam.

The resettlement of the Chinese squatter communities involved the movement of nearly half a million persons into security, but the bulk of those who were moved had no firm association with the areas from which they were removed. The apparent lesson to be gained in this respect is not only that affording security to uncommitted peasants is important. Just as importantly it is of considerable advantage to the established government that those who are moved should not be taken from regions with which they have ancestral connections. The immediate contrast which must be kept in mind is that between the squatter communities existing without social cohesion and waste-fully using their land, and the Vietnamese peasant de-voted to his ancestors' tombs and to the land which he tills.

The scale of the Malayan Emergency should be con-stantly kept in mind. Government superiority over the insurgents was never less than twelve or fifteen to one against a maximum enemy force of eight thousand. These eight thousand guerrillas had little opportunity to receive arms or supplies from outside Malaya and, although the Thai-Malayan border was never completely sealed off, they had only limited opportunities to make use of sanc-tuaries which could not be attacked by the government forces. Emphasis placed on the advantages which lay in the government's favour does not involve denigration of the military expertise demonstrated in Malaya. What it does do is to raise a cautionary warning against the all-too-ready assumption that the combating of liberation wars mounted by a Communist leadership will involve similar techniques throughout Southeast Asia. A generalization which may withstand analysis could be that the existence of similar military problems in different insurgency situations does not outweigh the profound importance of differing political circumstances.

The successes of the Malayan Government in first blunting and then eliminating the challenge posed by the Chinese insurgents during the Emergency has led to that conflict being seen as an exemplary guide to counter-guerrilla operations. So far as later developments in Viet-Nam are concerned, however, the American experience of operations against the Huk guerrillas in the Philippines may well have been of greater importance in shaping views of the nature of Communist-led revolt and of the necessary methods to combat it. The role which General Lansdale has played as an adviser to successive regimes and successive American ambassadors in South Viet-Nam stems directly from his important role as an adviser to President Magsaysay at the time the Huk revolt was effectively crushed.

However, it is not just that American personnel have transferred from the Philippines to a new theatre of insurgency in Viet-Nam. Indeed, the similarities between the Communist-led revolts of the Philippines and Viet-Nam appear, at first glance, to be much greater than is the case for Malaya and Viet-Nam. In both the Philippines and Viet-Nam an established authority faced the challenge of indigenous Communist-led groups which had developed during the Second World War and fought against the Japanese. Unlike the Chinese insurgents in Malaya, the Huks as Filipinos were members of the same ethnic group as the government which they attacked. Yet they were defeated in a remarkably short period and by Filipino troops who, even if they were advised by United States personnel, bore the brunt of the fighting which took place.

Yet as was the case with Malaya even the apparently greater similarities between the Philippines and Viet-Nam begin to seem less real once analysis goes beyond the superficial. The constant ingredients of a guerrilla challenge were present. Isolated government bases and forces were attacked by numerically larger guerrilla groups which faded away when facing major units. Guerrilla groups benefiting from the existence of peasant discontent were able to operate in the countryside which, while not always hostile to the government was uncertain of protection if any effort was made to refuse guerrilla demands for assistance. At no time however could the Huks claim to be the chief and most effective nationalist anti-colonial group in the same way that the Viet-Minh were able to do in Viet-Nam. Crucial to the way in which the government of the Philippines was able to overcome the Huk challenge was the fact that it was mounted against an established, independent government in a society where, whatever criticisms may be levelled against it, the national social structure remained intact.

Once the 'isolated' nature of the Huk challenge is recognized, it becomes easier to understand both the appeal of the Huks and the reasons for the revolt being crushed. The Huk challenge came from a particular area of the Philippines, one in which social tensions between landlord and peasant were great, and one in which the Huks as wartime guerrilla leaders had been able to demonstrate their dedication and courage. Emphasis placed on the social inequalities of the areas of central and southern Luzon which were the areas for the Huks' operations should not be taken as a suggestion that elsewhere no such inequalities existed. The nature of economic development in the Philippines has always led to economic power being held in the hands of a limited elite group. What was so important about such provinces as Pampanga and Tarlac in central Luzon was that in these regions the contrast between wealth and poverty and the strained nature of relationships between the landlords and the peasants were more dramatic than in other areas. Central Luzon, and to a lesser extent southern Luzon, provided ideal conditions for the expansion of sugar and copra plantations during the twentieth century. The development of these new and profitable enterprises did not lead to a wider distribution of wealth, but rather to increasing riches being concentrated in the hands of a traditional landlord class which now showed less and less concern to play its former role of protector of the peasantry. It was in such a situation that the twenties and thirties in the Philippines saw significant agrarian unrest in central Luzon, most notably with the formation of the Sadkalist movement in the middle thirties.

These developments provided an open invitation to Communist involvement, particularly when activity aimed at changing the existing social structure of the Philippines could have the additional significance of giving an opportunity to criticize the continued American presence in the islands. Yet when the involvement of the Communists is discussed it becomes apparent that both they, and the men who considered themselves to be socialists rather than Communists, had not at this stage developed any detailed theoretical critique of the problems which confronted them. The socialists and the Communists were often rivals and sometimes allies. Their power was limited, but it was often wasted in futile debate as to which of a number of alternative policies should be followed. Only with the advent of the Second World War were the leaders of the Communists in central Luzon able to move beyond political manoeuvring and efforts to stimulate strike action to build an active and disciplined guerrilla force. Able to combine its aims of bringing social change and fighting against the Japanese, the Huk army was, to a very real extent, the government of a large section of central Luzon. Under a talented leader, Luis Taruc, whose own account of the development of the Huk movement provides much of our information about wartime developments, the Huks were a formidable force when the war ended. The Philippines had suffered economically because of the Japanese occupation and its social fabric had sustained severe strains as a result of a division between those members of the elite who had opposed the Japanese and those who had collaborated with the occupying power.

In the tangle of Filipino politics in the post-war period the Huks at first indicated that they were prepared to engage in a peaceful contest for power with the other political parties. Seven of the Huk candidates for the Philippines Congress were elected in the 1946 elections; but the Congress, dominated by other parties which feared the intentions of the Huks, refused to seat them. This decision signalled the end to any possible peaceful accommodation between the Huks and the government in Manila. From 1946 until the collapse of the Huk armed movement in 1954 the contest was one in which military success became as important as political achievement.

Until 1950, however, it seemed that the Manila Government was unlikely ever to succeed in eliminating the challenge which the Huks posed. That this was so reflected not so much the invulnerability of the Huks as the inefficiency and general ineptitude of the central government. Scandal is no stranger to Filipino politics, but the post-war period with its combination of relief after the Japanese occupation and uncertainties about the future of the state seemed to call forth an ever-greater passion for gaining illicit wealth and lower political standards. The Philippines Army showed itself to be poorly led and ill-equipped to deal with a challenge which demanded other than conventional responses. Meanwhile the Huks showed that they had learned the lessons of their guerrilla activities against the Japanese. The Huk promises of improved conditions for the peasantry, particularly the right of the peasants to own their land, were not answered by any similar promises from the government. Supported by a disaffected peasantry, the Huks chose their own battle grounds and fought when they were sure of being able to inflict maximum casualties on the government troops. The problems of the government were aggravated by the way in which their forces showed little concern for the susceptibilities of the peasants, taking food and accommodation from them without payment.

There is continuing debate over the extent to which the

Huks were directed by Communist forces outside the Philippines and over the extent to which their relative success for some years is a reflection of Communist organizational abilities. On the first issue, it is extremely difficult to sustain an argument which would make the Huk revolt the direct outgrowth of policies conceived in Moscow, or elsewhere. The Communist identification of the leaders of the movement can be accepted, but this is no argument for external direction. Any argument which seeks to establish that such external direction took place must be based on the rather routine statements which the Soviet Government made in favour of the Huk revolt, and on the identification which many of the Huk leaders saw between their efforts and the world-wide Communist movement. The leaders of the Huks were sustained by their vision of international Communism, but they made their own decisions as to what policy should be followed in the Philippines. On the second point, it would be foolish to argue against the proposition that Communism had inspired the Huk leaders and that this political philosophy had, at the same time, seemed particularly appropriate to the condition in which the Filipino peasants were placed. Whatever the ultimate result of instituting a Communist regime may be, the appeal of a man who promises to end the arrangements which for generations have led to the progressive impoverishment of the peasants is difficult to resist. In the Philippines, in the late 1940s, only the Huks appeared dedicated to achieving social change.

At the beginning of 1950 the Huks had never seemed to be nearer their objective of playing a national rather than a regional role. Successive government operations against them had failed and the short-lived amnesty offered by President Quirino in 1948 had foundered on the differing interpretations of what was to be involved in the Huks ceasing to resist the government. By the end of the year the government was, by contrast, on the offensive and the hopes of the Huks to continue playing a significant role in determining the direction of Philippines development had already received some crushing blows. How had this transformation of the existing situation been achieved? A substantial body of literature has argued the attractive case that one remarkable man, Ramon Magsaysay, first as Secretary of Defence and later as President, wrought an administrative and political miracle and in doing so sapped whatever support the Huks had enjoyed. Much that was written about Magsaysay in the fifties now has a quaint and outdated air, with constant references to the defeat inflicted on the Huks as a blow against monolithic Communism, and with the suggestion that the promises of the period for genuine social reform were certain to come to fruition. Such accounts risk the development of an opposing and necessarily equally inaccurate view which gives little importance to Magsaysay's notable achievements. The truth does not necessarily lie in the middle, but any balanced assessment of why the Huks were defeated must take account of many factors over which neither Magsaysay nor the Huks had any control.

Ramon Magsaysay was an outstanding man and his personality, distinguished as it was by a degree of integrity which seemed foreign to the Philippines political scene, played a major part in the defeat of the Huks. He, like his Huk opponents, had had experience as a guerrilla during the war. Unlike the Huks, however, he believed that the existing society of the Philippines should and could be preserved. From the point of view of morale he succeeded in infusing the Philippines Government forces with a new enthusiasm. Much of this new feeling resulted from the personal example which Magsaysay provided. He toured dangerous regions with a minimal escort and attempted to show by example that the government did intend to take a real interest in the neglected problems of the peasantry. In the areas where morale blended with questions of technique, Magsaysay showed a similar able appreciation of the problems which the government faced. He demanded results from his soldiers and he made it clear that false reporting of achievements – a practice which had been common previously – would not be tolerated. There was brutality on the part of the army, and on the part of the guerrillas, but there is no need to dismiss the statements which Magsaysay made at the time that he endeavoured, with some success, to keep such excesses to a minimum. Also, though later events following Magsaysay's death did much to undermine his efforts for land reform, he made a start on this fundamental problem, and on the whole range of rural inequities, through the development of the Economic Development Corps (EDCOR), which was a section of the army with responsibilities for rural development.

Critics of the Philippines have stressed the extent to which Magsaysay was a creature of the United States. There is a basis to this criticism, not least when account is taken of the way in which, with Magsaysay's death, so many of the reforms which he had introduced withered away. But when American backing is taken fully into consideration, importance must still be allotted to this unusually able man. The record from other countries shows only too clearly that no amount of support provided by an outside power can, in itself, bring Southeast Asians to follow the path which the United States would prescribe.

If the importance of Magsaysay is allowed, the necessity still remains to analyse the features of the Huks' position in late 1950 which made the possibilities of success so limited. Possibly the most important had little to do with the 'objective conditions' of the situation in the Philippines, at least insofar as the Huks' difficulties were a reflection of special social and economic conditions in the area in which they were strongest. In October 1950 Magsaysay brought off the most significant intelligence coup of the entire campaign against the Huks. Acting on the basis of information provided by an informer, the Philippines Army and police were able to seize the Huk politburo headquarters in Manila along with Huk plans and the majority of the movement's political leadership. This was a colossal blow against the Huks and one from which they never recovered. It would be an over-simplification to suggest that after this success the defeat of the Huks was merely a matter of time. But it would be difficult, indeed, to overestimate the advantage which this development gave to the government. The destruction of the politburo made it possible for the Philippines Government to strike against the Huks without having to contend with some of their most able leaders.

As Magsaysay's campaigns gathered momentum many of the assumptions which the Huks had held began to look hollow. It is clear from the writings of Taruc and his close adviser William Pomeroy, an American who had deserted the United States Army to join the Huks, that the insurgents had an excessively optimistic vision of what could be achieved in the Philippines. Their vision was national, but the success which they achieved in central Luzon owed much to the particular conditions which obtained in that region. Social inequalities were to be found throughout Luzon, but in no other area were they so stark as in the Huk heartland, just to the north of Manila. The record of strikes and agitation which had been so characteristic of central Luzon during the thirties did not apply elsewhere. Moreover, despite the problems of tenant indebtedness which were widespread in other regions, the rural society outside central Luzon had not divided into such distinct, antagonistic classes. Class divisions were present in abundance, but these were divisions which were frequently accepted, while conflict, to the extent it existed, did not involve clashes between peasant and landlord but rather peasant and peasant, landlord and landlord. Social mobility was limited; awareness of inequalities existed; but Filipino society outside the Huk strongholds was not interested in, let alone ripe for, revolution. At the same time, the Filipino political scene did give evidence that able men could, on occasion, rise to the top without *ilustrado**

* The Spanish term used to describe the self-perpetuating Filipino elite which was made up of Spanish-speaking, and in part mixed descent, families who had an important economic and social position

connections. Magsaysay's case was exceptional, yet it would be wrong to suggest that Filipino society was entirely closed to those whose economic position was unsatisfactory.

By the time Magsaysay was elected President of his country in 1953, the hopes of the Huks that they could make any real challenge to the Philippines Government had been completely discounted. Progressively more successful raids against Huk bases brought increasing defections and betrayals. The promises of rural improvement had not been fully realized, but it did seem that the government was concerned to make good its intentions of improving the peasants' lot. Resettlement of Huk defectors away from their home territories in special areas on Mindanao appeared to provide some hope that the landless would become land owners.

The nature of history does not allow those who study it to state with certainty what would have happened had a particular event not occurred. For the Philippines the sudden death of Ramon Magsaysay in 1957 represents the kind of event where the wish for some gifts in historical hypothesizing becomes particularly strong. To what extent would the reforms which Magsaysay attempted to introduce have continued if he had not died in an air crash? To what extent had he ceased to believe, himself, in the possibility of rapid social change in the Philippines, even before outside observers had come to conclude that this was so? There are no sure answers to these questions. The only certain observations which may be made would stress the way in which the Philippines Government, under Magsaysay's impulsion, then his leadership, was successful in defeating the Huk challenge. That success did not carry with it any assurance of transformation. Peasant grievances remain and the Philippines economy is increasingly plagued by the threat of stagnation. The Huks were defeated, but not eliminated entirely. The promises of

under Spanish rule and continued to hold that position, with the addition of political power, under American control.

Magsaysay's regime, if they have not completely disappeared, have come to seem more difficult to achieve and more distant from realization than was the case in the pptimistic years of the mid fifties.

No matter how great the inequities which had brought the revolt of the Huks in central Luzon, and no matter how alienated the Chinese guerrillas of Malaya felt from the rest of the population, in neither instance of revolt could the insurgents lay claim to true nationalist identification. This was a fact of fundamental importance. The time which was required in both the Philippines and Malaya to overcome the challenges posed by these two revolts provides an indication of the slow and tedious techniques which must be used if success is to be achieved against guerrilla insurgents. The techniques which the respective governments used will remain of interest because of the success which each had. But if one is seeking to gain some understanding of why Communist-led revolts failed in the Philippines and Malaya but in part succeeded, and continue, in Viet-Nam, close attention must be given to the way in which neither the Huks nor Malaya's Chinese insurgents could convincingly claim the nationalist mantle. In Malaya the insurgents were prevented from doing this because of their ethnic identification. In the Philippines, despite the existence of widespread social problems, the Huks were confronted by a society which, as a whole, had not split into the sharply antagonistic groups which characterized their own particular area of influence. The contrasts which these countries, and their revolts, pose when compared with Viet-Nam has far too seldom been recognized.

# Chapter 7

# The Revolt that Half Succeeded

The events of the Second Indochinese War have tended to colour all descriptions of developments in Viet-Nam between 1946 and 1954 so that this period is too often seen as an *entr'acte* to later American involvement in Viet-Nam. Such a perspective is not unreasonable, particularly if it stresses the way in which the American presence in Viet-Nam, and the war in which American troops became major contestants, grew out of the unsatisfactory end to the First Indochinese War. The danger of looking only superficially at the 1946–54 period, however, lies in the fact that it then becomes all too easy to delineate both events and personalities in political blacks and whites; to draw all contrasts in terms of Communist or anti-Communist.

Unless recognition is given to the extent to which the Communist leaders of the revolt against French colonial power also had a nationalist character, an understanding of the history of Viet-Nam after the Second World War is impossible. It may appear a meaningless play upon words to note that Ho Chi Minh's nationalist solution for the problem of his country's relations with France was a Communist solution. The apparent tautology of this observation nevertheless reflects the manner in which a great many Vietnamese approached the problem. When the history of Viet-Nam during the period before the Second World War is considered, the attraction of Marxism is not difficult to recognize. Not only was political progress denied and political repression rife, but from an economic point of view the French administration of Viet-Nam appeared classically directed towards the interests of the colonial power with little, if any, consideration given to the economic interests of the colonized. The trunk road systems and the railways built in Viet-Nam were of little importance for the ordinary Vietnamese, who had neither the automobile to drive along the roads nor the necessary money to pay for his train fare.

In accepting that the group clustered about Ho Chi Minh combined both nationalist and Communist aims, there is no reason to dismiss the existence of other Vietnamese nationalists who rejected the totalitarian features of Communism and who were doubtful about its application to Vietnamese society. In very considerable contrast to the Viet-Minh, however, these men were unable to form a unified group to present an alternative to Ho Chi Minh's programme. Factionalism has been a persistent theme in Vietnamese history, and at a time when unity would have given the one opportunity for the non-Communist nationalists to provide any significant counterweight to the Viet-Minh, this unity was absent. Many commentators have dwelt on the way in which Ho and his lieutenants did not hesitate to use force to achieve their aims, killing Vietnamese opponents who refused to assist them. There is no call for an apologia to explain this brutal form of politics. The Viet-Minh were ruthless. There is little reason to think, however, that other Vietnamese groups rejected the concept of necessary violence in a revolutionary situation. What was so striking about the Viet-Minh's resort to terror and intimidation was its effectiveness. This was not the indiscriminate and unplanned violence of the earlier period of Vietnamese nationalist effort. The Viet-Minh leaders knew their goals and followed a total strategy in pursuing them. This observation applies both to the policies directed against their internal opponents and to the war which the Viet-Minh waged against the French.

The French, like the Dutch in Indonesia, were determined to regain control of their former colonial possessions in Indochina whether or not this meant fighting for them. When the Second World War came to a close, the situation in Viet-Nam was confused, and the events which followed upon the cessation of hostilities only added to that confusion. The Viet-Minh had made a bid for national power by proclaiming themselves the government of Viet-Nam in Hanoi. But in other sections of the country, particularly in the south, about Saigon, Viet-Minh control was not nearly so clearly established. For the whole of Viet-Nam the decision of the Allied powers to have a period in which British forces assumed control over the southern half of the country and Chinese Nationalist forces controlled the north did little to resolve the confusion. The British in the south acted to aid the French in their resumption of control. This early decisive event and the less highly developed form of the Communist organization in the south were later to aid the efforts of those Frenchmen who sought to promote a separatist state in the Cochinchina region – the southern third of South Viet-Nam. In the north, on the other hand, the Viet-Minh managed by some remarkable diplomatic improvisation to survive the Chinese occupation and even to remain established in Hanoi after the Chinese withdrew, looting the country systematically as they went.

With the departure of the Chinese forces from the north of Viet-Nam in early 1946 the opportunity existed for Vietnamese-French negotiations which might find some solution to what did not yet seem an intractable problem. Of all the 'might have beens' of recent Vietnamese history, few have excited as much discussion as the events of 1946. Could a different solution have been found if the French in Viet-Nam had not been directed by an uncompromising believer in the *gloire* of France? While the military commander in the south of Viet-Nam, General Leclerc, believed that accommodation could preserve French interests in Viet-Nam, his superior, Admiral d'Argenlieu, shared General de Gaulle's view that if Indochina did not belong to France it belonged to nobody. Was Ho Chi Minh the stumbling block to reasonable progress towards independence along the lines which other colonized

113

nations had followed? What is remarkable, in retrospect, is the extent to which Ho appeared to be genuinely prepared to compromise on some issues, always providing that the ultimate goal of independence was not put out of sight. In the conferences which took place in both Viet-Nam and France through 1946, Ho spoke with the authority which the Viet-Minh's expanding political and military activity provided. Although there is no doubt that the best approved Western practices were not followed by the Viet-Minh in the elections which took place, over the whole of Viet-Nam, early in 1946, Ho had through them confirmed his claim to be the most important politician in the country. With an increasing conviction in their strength, the Viet-Minh would not accept the basic demands of the French, which would have meant, in effect, an end to any hopes of real independence. Ho Chi Minh and his advisers were determined to have that independence. What might have happened if the French had not been so intransigent can never be proved. It could, perhaps, have included the emergence of a Viet-Nam with residual links to France.

As discussions proved fruitless, tension grew in Hanoi and Haiphong where the French and Vietnamese confronted each other. Clashes between Vietnamese and French in November 1946 led to the French cruiser *Suffren* shelling the Vietnamese quarter of Haiphong. The loss of life, particularly among civilians, was immense. In a few hours more than six thousand persons died. When the Vietnamese mounted their riposte against the French in Hanoi, during December, there was no longer any hope that a quick and peaceful solution could be found for Viet-Nam's problems. The failures of 1946 led to one of the most prolonged anti-colonial struggles in modern times. The revolt of the Vietnamese against French colonial power was dramatic, not merely because of the size to which the war eventually grew, but also because of the political revolution which accompanied the military revolt. Not only did the Viet-Minh war against the French lead to the establishment of an independent Vietnamese state, the savagery and duration of the war played a major part in confirming the nature of the state as a firmly Communist one, in which, at times, doctrine was followed with little thought for the implications of that doctrine in particular Vietnamese conditions.

In any attempt to understand why it was that the Viet-Minh forces were not defeated in Viet-Nam as the Communist-led guerrillas were in both Malaya and the Philippines, consideration must be given to the differences in scale. The Chinese guerrillas in Malaya probably never numbered more than eight thousand. In the Philippines, despite Huk propaganda claims, the anti-government guerrillas' hard-core fighting units did not exceed fifteen thousand. When the Viet-Minh had to face their first year of warfare against the French, they already had forty thousand trained troops. Scale again becomes important when one considers the areas over which the revolt against the French was mounted. During the war in Viet-Nam, the French were able to maintain control over the major urban centres, but from the very beginning of the conflict the French had to contend with the fact that attacks against their positions were likely to come throughout almost the whole of Viet-Nam. The main-force engagements were restricted to the north of the country, but the south was an accompanying running sore to the major infection in the regions of Tonkin and Annam, where the Viet-Minh had the best opportunities for fighting the guerrilla battles which they favoured. The sense of danger-filled isolation in the government outposts of the Mekong Delta region during the Viet-Minh war against the French has been brilliantly captured in Graham Greene's novel, *The Quiet American*.

The fact that the French were engaged on so many fronts throughout Viet-Nam serves to emphasize the extent to which this was a national battle for independence, in contrast to the efforts of the Communist guerrillas in Malaya and the Philippines. With the battle joined, there were few alternatives open to Vietnamese who were committed to ousting the French. For some, the alternative of exile seemed better than association with the colonial power or acceptance of Ho Chi Minh's leadership. The most prominent of the men who made this decision was Ngo Dinh Diem, who later became President of South Viet-Nam. An uncompromising Catholic, who would have no truck with Communism, or with its Vietnamese exponents who had murdered one of his brothers, he was, nevertheless, opposed to co-operation with the French. He found the solution to his personal dilemma in exile from his country. But this was not the choice that many other non-Communist nationalists made. These Vietnamese, some of them men of great ability, elected to fight with the Viet-Minh because of the genuine nature of its claim to be the one national force irrevocably committed to waging war against the French until independence was achieved.

Moreover, the contrast between the ascetic devotion of the Viet-Minh to their goals and the alternative Vietnamese leadership, backed by the French, was striking. Reluctant to provide their protégés with any significant power, the French attempted, time and again, to rally Vietnamese support for men who were largely discredited in the eyes of the politically conscious population. More firmly established in the southern (Cochinchina) region than elsewhere, the French at first attempted to gain support for a separate Cochinchinese state. When this policy failed, a decision was taken to build up a nationalist alternative to the Viet-Minh by working through the Vietnamese emperor, Bao Dai. It may be that the widespread criticism Bao Dai has received from so many writers is far from fully deserved. What does appear certain is that the French should have realized the disadvantages associated with an attempt to capitalize on the necessarily restricted appeal of the last representative of the Vietnamese royal house. Ever since Ham Nghi's flight from the court at Hue in 1885, the Vietnamese emperors had been puppets of the French colonial government. Bao Dai himself, despite his high hopes in the thirties of becoming a worthy servant of his people, had bowed to French insistence that he should occupy no more than a symbolic role on the throne, isolated from his people and distracted from worldly demands by frequent hunting trips. What is more, Bao Dai's position in the post-war period had become particularly ambiguous, since he had at first agreed to work with the Viet-Minh and then renounced this association in favour of exile in Hong Kong.

When, after considerable hesitation on the part of both the French and Bao Dai, the decision was made to work politically against the Viet-Minh through a quasi-independent State of Viet-Nam, the difficulties which this entity faced seemed almost insurmountable. Bao Dai himself had been reluctant to associate his name with the French because of the extent to which the colonial power retained its control over the major instruments of government. That the French budged from their intransigent position at all reflected their concern, as the war dragged on, to gain the maximum international support for their efforts against what they were at this time describing as yet another instance of the machinations of international Communism. But the Bao Dai solution never really had any chance of success so long as the French refused to transfer real power to the Vietnamese. French commercial interests, particularly in rubber and rice, remained strongest in that southern area of Viet-Nam which could most reasonably be described as under French military control. French businessmen and long-established incumbents of the colonial civil service applied strong pressure on the French home government to prevent the State of Viet-Nam from gaining any real degree of independence. And in the French-controlled areas of the south there were sufficient numbers of Vietnamese, particularly amongst those whose families had grown rich during colonial times, who were ready to serve in positions which gave some prestige through name if not through authority. Whatever else Bao Dai could do, the refusal of the French to accord him real power ensured that he could not lead a successful battle against the Viet-Minh revolutionaries.

While political manoeuvring took place with the aim of establishing an anti-Communist, nationalist Vietnamese state, still subservient to France, the military conflict dragged on, with no sign that France was able to best the Viet-Minh troops in any definitive fashion. Myths have grown up, promoted by advocates for each side in the conflict, which have obscured much of the reality of events. Supporters and spokesmen for the Democratic Republic of Viet-Nam have presented an account of the war in which the dedicated zeal of poorly armed men, inspired by the goal of national independence, brought the Viet-Minh ever closer to annihilating the French. Commentators sympathetic to the French point of view have insisted that the French troops were not defeated on the battlefields of Indochina, but rather in Paris, where ineffectual governments provided insufficient support and a divided population failed to provide the essential morale necessary to the successful prosecution of the war. Grains of truth lie within each of these explanations; but in themselves they are too simple.

General Vo Nguyen Giap, the Viet-Minh military leader, has had sufficient military success to be able to eschew much of the routine propaganda which is published under his name, and in relation to him by his government. The needs of the state, presumably, demand the furnishing of this material, but his capabilities are not really in doubt among informed observers of Viet-Nam. What is in doubt is that Giap is omniscient and omnipotent in military matters. The record of the First Indochinese War assured him a place in military history, but it also revealed that he was fallible. Equally, it does not detract from the capacities of the troops who fought under Giap to note that they did not always move forward with a total dedication. In fact, as an able military historian has recently pointed out, not the least remarkable aspect of the climactic battle for Dien-Bien-Phu was the way in which Giap found it necessary, during the battle itself, to engage in political indoctrination to eliminate hesitance among his troops.

When the military conflict between the French and the Vietnamese is viewed in human rather than super-human terms, there remains reason to take account of the very real achievement of Giap and his troops. General Giap did not start life as a soldier. He studied law and politics. Before joining the anti-French guerrillas led by Ho Chi Minh, he was a teacher of history. He learnt his military craft in the Second World War period; when he first came to command more than company-sized forces, his experiences had scarcely prepared him for the task which he undertook. A natural thoroughness and caution seem to have played their part in his campaigns up to 1950. He observed the fundamental rules of guerrilla warfare against a more powerful enemy – striking only when his forces had either numerical superiority or overwhelming advantage from surprise; withdrawing in the face of stronger forces in pursuit. His caution left him in 1950 and 1951, when he slipped from observing these classic rules for success to make classic mistakes. He fought with his lines of supply extended; knowing the importance of a supporting civilian population, he nevertheless engaged the French in regions where the Viet-Minh had not been successful in gaining the people to their side; on occasion, he allowed his troops to mass before enemy positions in areas which were within easy reach of French aerial support, with resultant high casualties. It was mistakes of this sort which led to Giap's more careful campaigning of late 1952 and early 1953 when the end of the war still seemed far away.

The main-force battles, however, while of great importance for the various phases of the Franco-Viet-Minh conflict, did not, by any means, reflect the whole picture of developments. The Viet-Minh had had to work clandestinely in the 1930's, and this experience was of the greatest importance in efforts to gain the allegiance of the countryside, even within regions that the French claimed to control. The late Bernard Fall has shown how shallow were French claims to effective control in so much of Viet-Nam. The lack of an overt Viet-Minh military presence was no guarantee that the Communist-led forces were not active within villages. From the Viet-Minh's point of view, the active co-operation, if possible, and the coerced co-operation, if necessary, of the rural population was as important as being able to recruit troops for main-force units. They had their own experience to build on and were fully aware of the efforts which the Chinese Communist forces had made in this sphere of guerrilla campaigning.

Above all, the Viet-Minh cadres who worked to ensure support among the rural population had two great advantages. Convinced of the value of their own cause, they worked with a population which, after decades of disorientation, was predisposed to change. The old values which had been personified in the emperor at Hue, and through him in the traditional mandarinate, had been shattered. The French had once represented unassailable power, but the impression of invincibility had passed. Into this situation came men of their own race and culture who were prepared to work with the peasants and who promised at the same time the alleviation of problems which had pressed upon the rural population for generations – not least the promise of greater land rights and elimination of the all-too-frequent periods of food shortage which have long plagued the northern sections of Viet-Nam. The sceptical comments of those who suggest that such promises from Communists would be rejected by the peasantry miss the point. Not only is it clear that a promise has regularly been sufficient incentive for political affiliation; at a rather more sophisticated level, the very fact that men with political aims were now working with the peasants, who had so often been ignored in the changes of government and regime, was important in leading to peasant support.

The other great advantage which the cadres had in their

task related to the undoubted national element in their programme for change. Viet-Nam, unlike so many other Third World countries, has long possessed a sense of national identity. Practical and political considerations acted to thwart real national unity throughout much of Vietnamese history, but the ideal of unity remained. When, after the French forward movement took place in the nineteenth century, isolated groups of Vietnamese continued to fight on, they did so in terms of some ill-defined, but nonetheless firmly held, vision of an independent country.

In the period of the Viet-Minh's war against the French it was of the greatest importance that those who worked to gain peasant support should be able to speak in terms of national aims as well as local problems. In Viet-Nam, as elsewhere in Southeast Asia, one may at times speak of the bulk of the peasantry as apolitical and often unready to respond to those who wish them to participate in movements directed to goals outside their villages. Yet unless one is to fall back on the obviously unsatisfactory argument that peasant co-operation with the Viet-Minh was entirely the result of coercion, it becomes essential to take account of the factors which could bring widespread involvement in the conflict. Amongst these, the appeal to the importance of a national struggle against colonialism was of deep significance. Both for the First and Second Indochinese Wars, a consistent feature of Western analysis has been the reluctance of many commentators to accept that ideals as well as organization have played their part in sustaining the efforts of those who fought first against the French and then against the Americans. It is salutary to reflect that the lack of any widely held ideal, other than a commitment to self-preservation, may explain the inability of so many of the anti-Communist Vietnamese movements to match both the political and military success of their enemies.

Uncertainty of aim and lack of support from the home population in France sapped the French military effort and showed that, whatever France's justificatory rhetoric, there was no burning ideal guiding the colonial power's war effort. There had, perhaps, been such an ideal at the beginning. General de Gaulle and Admiral d'Argenlieu regarded French glory as absolutely committed to the preservation of the overseas empire, and in particular of *notre Indochine*. The most remarkable of the French commanders in Viet-Nam, General de Lattre de Tassigny, who for a limited period instilled a new spirit in the French forces fighting in Indochina, held a clear vision of France's imperial role and fought for it with a devotion inherited from his martial ancestors, losing his only son, a young lieutenant, in the process. But for all the military bravery displayed in Viet-Nam, the French nation's heart was not in the struggle. Political division in Paris prevented firm policies, whether increased commitment in Viet-Nam or speedy concessions to end the war. European problems weighed more heavily than those of the Far East. And there was a substantial proportion of Frenchmen on the political left who were utterly opposed to French troops fighting in Indochina.

In Viet-Nam itself, the French community, both official and private, often appeared more interested in opportunities for personal enrichment than in participation in the war. The opportunities for increasing private wealth through an officially sanctioned exchange manipulation of the Indochinese piastre against the French franc only further encouraged corruption. Saigon, always a city which had catered adequately for men with less than entirely honest principles, now became a by-word in Southeast Asia for its opportunities to make quick fortunes with a minimum of official interference.

The opposition which was mounted against the Franco-Viet-Minh War in France and the role played by the French Communist Party in terms of strikes and sabotage against shipments of *matériel de guerre* has led to the often quoted argument that France lost the Indochinese War in Paris. The judgement is simplistic and erroneous. Political instability and lack of enthusiasm for the war played their part in bringing the French defeat. But an attempt to separate events in France from those in Indochina fails to take account of the total nature of any major military conflict. The cry of wars lost by politicians at home has been heard over the centuries, from the losing side and their supporters. The beauty of the argument, for those who advance it, lies in its hypothetical nature. Since France was split by the war, it seems eminently reasonable to argue that without political division there would have been a very different outcome. As an unproven possibility such an hypothesis stands outside argument. As a certain assumption the argument has no intellectual status. What can be noted with certainty is that the French domestic situation was an important contributory factor in the Viet-Minh's ultimate success. That the forces led by Ho Chi Minh should have tried to take advantage of French hesitations and divisions should scarcely be surprising. The Viet-Minh fought with the conviction that a long war would further divide a nation which could not, in the long run, sustain a military conflict in which the aims being pursued and the benefits to be gained were unclear. To see this Viet-Minh analysis as peculiarly Communist is a misunderstanding of the situation. A long war fought with the hope of sapping the opponent's will is much more correctly seen as an old weapon in the armory of a militarily weak state. To count upon division of the home population playing a part in affecting the performance of troops in the field does not, qualitatively or even strategically, appear so very different from seeking to end the Second World War through massive bombing raids directed as much against civilians as against strictly military targets.

A further danger associated with the view that France lost the Indochinese War in Paris stems from the manner in which such an analysis tends to disguise the extent to which the Viet-Minh had succeeded in gaining control in the countryside of Viet-Nam, even if before Dien-Bien-Phu the issue of whose main-force units were the strongest still had to be resolved. By 1953 it was correct to speak of an uneasy stalemate in the war between the French and Viet-Minh regulars. After his defeats in 1950 and 1951, General Giap had reorganized his forces and undertaken less ambitious operations, strengthened by the equipment which the victorious Chinese Communist Government shipped across the border in increasing quantities. On the French side, the military command had begun to see the value of increased efforts to achieve population control through pacification techniques, and the need to counter their enemy's guerrilla activity by the use of similarly mobile unconventional forces. But while the French military leaders pondered how to lure the Vietnamese into a major conventional battle, in which it was believed that French logistic superiority and more advanced equipment would triumph, the Viet-Minh cadres continued to improve their hold over the countryside. General Navarre, the last of the French military commanders in the Indochinese War, has emphasized in his aptly titled book, *Agonie de l'Indochine*, the extent to which his forces fought in a country where they had no permanent control over most of the settled land and no support from the population outside urban centres. The French in Viet-Nam used an expression which, from their point of view, adequately described the situation. They spoke of the countryside as having become 'rotten'.

In late 1953, after seven years of inconclusive war, the French high command in Viet-Nam sought to bring a decisive change in affairs which would, in one blow, destroy the Viet-Minh military threat and place France on the political offensive. The battle which resulted from this thinking was that of Dien-Bien-Phu. Initially, Navarre saw the occupation of Dien-Bien-Phu, a valley hard by the Laotian border, as a way to ensure that Giap's forces could not move at will in and out of Laos, as well as an opportunity to deal the enemy a major blow. But confronted with greater Viet-Minh forces than they had anticipated, the French high command were to see the battle for Dien-Bien-Phu become a symbol of the French capacity to survive in Indochina.

The military folly of this battle may be mitigated but can never be redeemed by the courage shown on both sides. For the French the battle was a disaster in which the inability of their military leaders to recognize the capacities of those whom they confronted cost them dearly. The French high command underestimated how many troops the Viet-Minh would send against them; they failed to take due account of the artillery available to the enemy; and they severely underestimated the logistic capabilities of an enemy which made as much use of manpower for transporting supplies as of more modern methods. Even the site of Dien-Bien-Phu was beset with disadvantages, as the French troops found that the soil was poorly suited for the construction of trench and shelter complexes.

For the forces directed by General Giap, the battle of Dien-Bien-Phu was a political and military triumph. As the battle entered its most vital phase the Geneva Conference had already begun its deliberations, in which the future of Viet-Nam was one of the most vital questions under consideration. The challenge was one which Giap recognized and to which he responded. Using artillery techniques which had served the Chinese well in Korea, the Viet-Minh were able to set their guns in forward positions where the French least expected them to be. The battle was one of attrition, with the Vietnamese troops suffering heavier casualties than the French as they moved forward relentlessly, grinding down the defenders and ringing their dug-in positions with a network of trenches. But the high military cost was entirely acceptable to Giap, and to his fellow Viet-Minh leaders. The French had made the battle a test of their will and capacity, and they failed. Despite the growing American financial involvement in the war against the Viet-Minh, the United States had not been prepared to give military assistance in the form of bombing strikes against Giap's positions, which might have reversed the tide. The French position was finally overcome on 8 May 1954.

As the battle for Dien-Bien-Phu took place against the background of the Geneva Conference the success of the Viet-Minh became a necessity, to ensure that no doubts would be held about the Democratic Republic of Viet-Nam's will to survive and its capacity to fight in doing so. The defeat of the French in this epic battle ensured the Viet-Minh's partial political success, but in a world tensely divided along cold war lines it proved impossible for the Communist-led Vietnamese to gain their ultimate aim: total control of Viet-Nam.

The legal implications of the Geneva Conference are still being debated. From the point of view of political analysis, the best judgement of the decisions written into the Geneva Accords was made by Bernard Fall when he argued that, like Panmunjom in Korea, the ceasefire agreements which the French achieved were the best that could be accomplished. Few more convincing insights into the truth of this observation exist than the comments on the Geneva Accords which the French Prime Minister, Mendès-France, made immediately after the end of the conference. Accused by his political opponents of giving away more to the Viet-Minh than was necessary in the Accords, Mendès-France noted that the opposite was, in fact, the case. The Viet-Minh had settled for a temporary division of Viet-Nam at the seventeenth parallel when in reality all of the provinces between the seventeenth and thirteenth parallels could be regarded as long-term centres of support for the anti-French forces.

Argument will long continue over the exact significance of the Geneva Accords and the extent to which these unsigned agreements, chiefly concerning the French Government and the Democratic Republic of Viet-Nam, were binding upon, or conferred an existence on, a separate South Vietnamese state. This legal debate, however, only goes part of the way in explaining why the Accords were so singularly unsuccessful in bringing conflict in Viet-

Nam to an end. At the Geneva Conference, to the North Vietnamese leaders' bitter regret, the Soviet Union and China preferred to act more as great powers seeking to prevent an erosion of world peace than as dedicated supporters of the Viet-Minh position. Instead of backing the Viet-Minh claim to rule the whole of Viet-Nam, Molotov and Chou En-lai were ready to counsel compromise, at least for a period. In particular, the Viet-Minh agreed, under the pressure exercised by Russia and China, to accept a regroupment of opposing forces and the temporary division of Viet-Nam, on the understanding that during 1956 an election would be held throughout Viet-Nam to decide the issue of reunification. After the long bitter years of war, only a genuine expectation on the part of the Viet-Minh leaders that this election would in fact take place can explain their readiness to accept a further waiting period. Contrary to suggestions by some writers, the Viet-Minh were not totally exhausted after Dien-Bien-Phu. This was shown by their brilliant operation against the French mobile column Number 100 which came after the famous siege battle. Given the degree of power which they had exercised in the south and the fact that a substantial number of political cadres had remained in the southern areas after the withdrawal of main-force units to the north, the Viet-Minh had every reason to believe that they would gain by a vote the fruits of their earlier military struggles.

But France, who was to have played an essential role in ensuring that the 1956 elections took place, decided to be rid completely of responsibility for Viet-Nam; the regime which began so shakily in the south now had a new protector instead, the United States. When, with United States support and encouragement, the South Vietnamese President Ngo Dinh Diem refused to participate in joint elections in 1956, it was certain that the Indochinese War would begin again.

No other Southeast Asian state waged such a bitter and

prolonged battle for independence against a colonial power as did Viet-Nam. The anti-colonial revolt in Indonesia had brought periods of sustained violence, but never on the scale that was so characteristic of Viet-Nam. Faced with French reluctance to grant independence, men who had a long background of resistance to the colonial power's control were able to weld together a political and military apparatus which could survive a long war without neglecting political objectives.

To have stressed, as this chapter has done, that Ho's political identification is to be understood in terms of the way in which Communism and nationalism were parts of a whole in his outlook, does not solve the moral dilemmas of an outside observer in Vietnamese affairs. The Viet-Minh's victory over the French was the success of Viet-Nam's most powerful and successful nationalist group – which was, at the same time, Communist-led. With the war's end, there were men whose nationalism was not in dispute, including a number who had fought on the Viet-Minh side, who chose to oppose the expansion of northern control over the south of the country. Was the only way to meet the needs of these men, and such minority groups as the Vietnamese Catholics, through the establishment of a southern state which was cast in the role of an anti-Communist bastion, an advance base in the containment of China?

One can only speculate about the nature of the state which might have emerged had Ho Chi Minh gained control over all of Viet-Nam in 1954 or 1956. But it is possible to enumerate with some precision the reasons why Ho and his lieutenants could not leave their anti-colonial revolt at a half-way point. These men, no less than any other Vietnamese nationalists, were committed to the ideal of a single Vietnamese state. Politically, a divided Viet-Nam cut across historical ideals and the present facts of a situation in which no geographical dividing line had existed in the conduct of the war or in the composition of the Viet-Minh leadership. Economically, Viet-Nam, even in earlier periods of political division, has been one, with the over-crowded north and centre dependent upon the rice surplus of the south.

It would be blind romanticism to ignore the importance which Communist doctrine and organization played in the success of the Viet-Minh War. Equally, the nature of the Viet-Minh regime which came to power in North Viet-Nam cannot be understood unless due consideration is given to the actions of that regime in such fields as the disastrous and mistaken land reform campaign which be-gan in 1953, and which cost so many thousands of lives. But the harsh and necessary fact about Viet-Nam and the Viet-Minh War, one which was so often misunderstood when the war ended, was the extent to which the revolt which began in 1945 had a national character. Refusal to accept this fact and failure to see in North Viet-Nam any-thing more than an extension of China, led to mis-estima-tions about Viet-Nam once the United States decided to involve itself in the affairs of the region. The divided Viet-Nam which emerged after 1954 was ruled by two govern-ments, each of which believed that it had a right to control over the whole country. The belief that right, integrity and nationalism could only be found south of the seven-teenth parallel led to the ultimate confrontation of North Viet-Nam and the United States in what, throughout its duration, has been a sadly misunderstood conflict.

# Chapter 8

# The Myth-Ridden War

No war in history has been the subject of such widespread contention as that which developed in Viet-Nam in the years after the Geneva Settlements of 1954. The existence of a mass media capable of providing intense and almost immediate coverage of the war's drama has played a major, if yet far from fully analysed, part in directing public interest to the political and moral dilemmas raised by the conflict. Sociologists and historians are likely to argue in the future on the extent to which the unpopularity of the Viet-Nam War has sprung from a general presence of youthful discontent in the developed countries of the world, most notably in the United States. Was the war the cause of the alienation from established values which seems to have been greater than anything experienced in the past century? In a war which has brought forth passionate defenders and passionate critics of official policy, American commentators seem agreed that the war in Viet-Nam has been the most unpopular waged in their nation's history. In these circumstances there should be no surprise at the extent to which the war has brought into being an extraordinary range of myths and misconceptions. These have emerged from both the left and the right. The tragedy has been that governments have established their policies within the framework of these myths, which have been susceptible to criticism, and have apparently been unwilling to abandon the misconceptions, even after they had been proved to be false.

The nature of the partition of Viet-Nam which followed upon the conclusion of the First Indochinese War has become a matter of sharp disagreement in any discussion of the war. While it is probably an excessive simplification to suggest that only those who have supported the American position in Viet-Nam have seen a permanent division of Viet-Nam following quite naturally upon the discussions which accompanied the Geneva Accords, and to see only critics of the war holding a contrary view, such has frequently been the case. The problem which has resulted from the first view of the meaning of the Accords and negotiations at the Geneva Conference has been the unreadiness of those who have argued for the separate existence of South Viet-Nam to comprehend the extent to which the Viet-Minh between 1946 and 1954 had waged their struggle for the whole of Viet-Nam. Failure to recognize this factor in the situation has led to mis-estimations of the most profound kind as to the extent to which the Communist leadership saw both national and nationalist interests involved in their exclusion from the south.

The fundamental myth which has bedevilled official American views of developments in Viet-Nam in the years after 1954 has been the belief in the possibility that two Vietnamese states could exist peacefully within the geographical territory of Viet-Nam. The decision to support Ngo Dinh Diem's government, taken in 1954, revealed virtually no awareness of the way in which the war that the Viet-Minh had fought against the French had been conceived in national terms. By backing Diem, and his successors, the United States took up an option which always held the threat of war. This is not a matter of morals, but a question of fact. The Viet-Minh's major military efforts had been concentrated in the north and centre of Viet-Nam; but their interest in the south had been real and had been demonstrated in the extent to which the Viet-Minh established a major presence in the countryside. The paradox of accepting the myth that it was possible to partition Viet-Nam without the gravest risk lay in the way that United States representatives in South Viet-Nam were fully aware that the Diem government cherished its own hope of eventually controlling the whole of Viet-Nam's territory.

The consequences which flowed from accepting the view that peaceful partition was a possibility were tremendous. On the military side it led to the belief that the only serious challenge which could face the southern regime would be in terms of an externally mounted invasion. American advisers imbued with memories of the Korean War directed their efforts towards the training of a conventional army ready to resist the southward movement of regular North Vietnamese troops. The level of proficiency which these advisers were able to instil was far from high. More to the point, however, this concentration of conventional forces revealed an unreadiness to realize that partition had not ended the existence below the seventeenth parallel of political cadres who were committed to the ultimate triumph of the Viet-Minh regime.

The political consequences of the thinking behind partition were, if anything, more dramatically damaging to the hopes of the United States for its protégé. The myth brought about thinking which chose to see all nationalist sentiment located south of the seventeenth parallel, while Communism was only to be found in the north. Just as had been the case during the First Indochinese War, the subtleties and complexities of the relationship between Communism and nationalism were once more ignored or misunderstood. Because Ngo Dinh Diem was a bitter enemy of Communism, this became a guarantee of his ability, even when during the closing years of his rule the evidence became increasingly strong of his failure to understand, let alone control, the opposition which had developed to his position.

The debates which have dominated discussion in the West of the Viet-Nam War have too often failed to recognize myths or to make critical analyses of assumptions which have often had only the most dubious basis of fact for their formulation. In the aftermath of an American decision not to continue the fight for a military victory it has been inevitable that the advocates of such a 'victory' have assembled their arguments for the proposition that, had restrictions dictated by political considerations not been applied, the military in Viet-Nam could have successfully brought the war to a conclusion in which North Viet-Nam sued for peace, ready to accept the independence of the south. The beauty of this argument lies in the extent to which it cannot be resolved by any rational means of debate. Speculation may be profitable to illuminate the counter-factual possibilities which can so often seem of greater attraction than what actually took place, but history, while it must concern itself with possible alternatives to the actual progression of events, cannot become preoccupied with those alternatives to the exclusion of examining what did eventuate. In Viet-Nam, for a variety of complex internal and external considerations, the United States could not commit unlimited numbers of troops to fight for an unlimited period. This was always a limitation which was likely to operate to restrict American effectiveness, and policies were conceived within this framework. The escalation which came in 1965 revealed a miscalculation both about the strength of the enemy which the United States and its allies confronted, and of that enemy's own commitment not to give up the pursuit of its basic goals.

Although it is easy to discern myth-making on the part of the critics of the United States involvement, the course which the war has followed and the terms in which it was justified make a review of the errors of the policy-makers all-important. Beyond the basic false assumptions which grew from the fundamental myth, the student of Vietnamese affairs encounters instance after instance in which decisions of the greatest importance appear to have been taken with only the slightest regard for the *Vietnamese* factors involved. The decision to support Ngo Dinh Diem and then to back his rejection of the elections proposed under the Geneva Accords as a means of unifying Viet-Nam is a notable example of this failure to treat Vietnamese problems in terms of the local factors involved.

Quite clearly, Ngo Dinh Diem was devoted to his own image of an independent Viet-Nam. But his handicaps in seeking to implement that vision were formidable. As a Catholic he came from the minority of the Vietnamese population which has so consistently been regarded by the majority as 'strangers in their own country'. As an uncompromising opponent of French colonial power in Viet-Nam he showed his opposition not in terms of association with the battle which was actually waged against the French, but rather in terms of exile from where he adopted the view of 'a plague on both your houses' in relation to both the Communists and those non-Communist Vietnamese who were prepared to collaborate with the French. A man from north-central Viet-Nam, when he came to power in South Viet-Nam – an area with strong regional tendencies – he sought to bolster his position through reliance on northern and central Vietnamese, particularly the Catholic element amongst them. It is small wonder that even President Eisenhower believed that in the immediate post-Geneva period Ho Chi Minh was the most popular man in the whole of Viet-Nam.

Since Ngo Dinh Diem was a far from popular figure, some convincing explanation must be found which provides an account of why it should have been that Diem was left unchallenged by those who, as the Viet-Minh, had fought for so long to gain control over the whole of the country. Once again, passion as much as evidence is apparent in so many of the explanations which are put forth. The Geneva Accords had provided for elections under international supervision to determine the future reunification of the country. One major point at issue is whether or not those in Hanoi agreed to this provision with any real conviction that the elections would take place. Did they, as some commentators would suggest, accept that the elections would not eventuate and plan instead for the long-term seizure of power through armed force? Personal views on the nature of the war once again seem to be the determinant of attitudes on this matter. The difficulty with the view that the North Vietnamese never believed in the elective process is that at the time the Accords were concluded there seemed no reason for the Viet-Minh leadership not to believe that the French Government would assume the responsibilities laid down which called upon it to assist in implementing elections. Baulked, as the Hanoi regime saw itself, from gaining its just deserts by the Geneva Conference, the prospect of elections leading peacefully to what had not yet been gained through the war was far from an unacceptable proposition. Moreover, while the northern half of Viet-Nam was stronger than the south, it still had to face major problems. The damage of nearly nine years of war could not be ignored. Even more importantly the disastrous land reform programmes introduced in 1953 had led to substantial opposition to the regime in certain important regions of the country. The brutal and savage repression which had accompanied the 'reform' had led to severe peasant discontent which, if it did not threaten the fabric of the state, had at least left it under considerable stress.

By the end of 1954, however, there was no longer any likelihood that the French would play a role in promoting elections. When Diem and his United States sponsors made it clear that under no circumstances would they agree to an electoral process the northern regime was faced with the need to reassess its strategy. By 1956 it was evident that a new era had begun in which the failure of the Geneva Accords to settle the overall future of Viet-Nam was temporarily disguised. The regime based in Hanoi was working to consolidate its position. There were similar preoccupations on the part of the Diem government in the south. It was in this condition of temporary stalemate that the emergence of an insurrection designed to overthrow the Saigon Government took place. The reason for its emergence and the character which it had remain amongst the most heatedly debated issues in the whole controversy associated with the war.

The position adopted by the United States Government

and those who have supported its policies has been that the southern insurgency was planned and implemented at the direction of the Hanoi regime. As such, it was 'aggression by proxy' which reflected not the discontent of members of the population with a repressive and unpopular administration, but rather the machinations of a rapacious Communist government determined to gain by stealth what it had not achieved by open war. The strength of this particular argument lies in the fact that there were former Viet-Minh cadres in the south who came to form the essential base for the insurgency which broke out. The weakness of the argument lies in the suggestion that there was nothing in Ngo Dinh Diem's rule which made likely some form of overt protest against his policies. For the reality of Diem's rule in South Viet-Nam, once he had successfully neutralized the politico-religious sects which had disputed his power, was that through its harshness and single-minded pursuit of security by means of repression of all opposition, whatever its ideological identification, the regime ensured the growth of opposition.

Although the proposition has been advanced that Diem's major mistake was a failure to be firmer than he was, it is difficult to envisage that such a possible alternative policy would have achieved a strengthening of the Saigon regime. Lacking a successfully promoted state philosophy and without any credible claim to national leadership, either for the peasants or for the uncommitted bourgeois and intellectual elements of the urban centres, Ngo Dinh Diem's regime could neither match the reforming promises of his Communist-led opponents who spoke of land reform, nor provide the apparatus to establish a centralized state control of the sort which enabled those who ruled in Hanoi to survive the brutal errors of internal government made between 1953 and 1956. Yet when the errors of Diem's policies have been sketched, the question still remains as to why it was that opposition emerged at the time which it did, and in the form that it took.

On one point there seems little dispute. The backbone

of the movement which begun to undermine Diem's tenuous grip on power was the reserve of former Viet-Minh cadres who had remained in the south after 1954. In some areas of South Viet-Nam the power of these men had been completely obscured as they accepted the need to bide their time. In other regions, the former cadres had never lost their power over the peasantry. It is salutary to note some of the comments made by President Ngo Dinh Diem's brother, Ngo Dinh Nhu, in the final years of his brother's regime; quite in contrast to the propaganda claims which had been made so often before, he admitted that there were villages in South Viet-Nam that had never passed out of the hands of the Communists. These cadres possessed a number of powerful psychological weapons when the time came to challenge the Diem regime. As former members of the Viet-Minh they represented that force which had fought so successfully against the French, even if it had failed to achieve all its aims. They were, even if distantly and somewhat tenuously, the men who embodied the spirit of Ho Chi Minh. Ho's identification as the great hero of the anti-colonial struggle survived through the sixties, despite the transformation of the struggle in Viet-Nam from a civil war to a conflict involving international forces. In the late fifties this identification may well have been even stronger.

Finally, the mistakes of the Diem regime, and its failure to make any positive move to match the promises of reforms which the re-emerging Viet-Minh cadres were making, left the cadres unchallenged as the one significant group which showed an interest in the peasants. Some commentators have drawn attention to the contrast between the offers of land reform made by the insurgents in the south and the realities of land reform in the north in which the mistakes of Ho's government were so monumental that the regime had to make a public admission of its errors. The Diem government constantly stressed the errors of its northern competitor. But what it emphasized were abstractions for the southern peasant. He might be told that life was harsh north of the seventeenth parallel. He knew that it was difficult in the south and that he paid rent to an absentee landlord who showed little if any interest in his position. He knew, too, that during the First Indochinese War the Viet-Minh had in fact redistributed land, and that men who were directly linked with these earlier acts of land distribution now promised to do the same again. In the cities the educated and the wealthy knew of the 'political re-education centres' in which for every Vietnamese Communist held under detention there were at least as many non-Communists whose mistake had been to become identified as disenchanted with Diem's rule.

As the first five years of Diem's rule drew to a close the state of security in the countryside declined rapidly as Diem's opponents, concentrating their attacks on officials and employees of the government, began to demonstrate that short of the actual presence of sizeable armed forces no region or person was safe from their attacks. The degree of organizational skill shown in this emerging threat to President Diem's control and the fact that former Viet-Minh cadres led the activity have been cited as convincing evidence that the whole operation was directed and instigated from Hanoi. If the view that Viet-Nam is properly considered as one and not two states is accepted, the fact that there should have been northern involvement in the growing southern insurgency ceases to be surprising, whatever views might be held of the moral issues involved. From the point of view of the men who had fought for so long to place their imprint on the political future of Viet-Nam the continued existence of a foreign-backed state in the south was an affront. Yet even if the view of the rightful existence of two Vietnamese states is accepted, there are certain problems about the way in which the southern insurrection began which must be considered, if not necessarily solved. For the government in Hanoi has steadfastly denied that it promoted the developments in South Viet-Nam in the period before December 1960 when it gave its approval to the foundation of the National Liberation Front for South Viet-Nam.

It is a truism of Western commentary on countries of the Communist world that statements from the governments of those countries must never be taken at face value. In the case of North Viet-Nam, the consistent refusal of the Hanoi Government to admit the presence of its armed forces south of the seventeenth parallel provides a typical example of what Western observers have come to see as the norm of Communist deception. But how to judge the denials of Hanoi of its involvement in the south before 1960 is another question. At one level there is clear evidence of the way in which the government of North Viet-Nam sought to make propaganda capital out of the rising level of opposition to Diem's position. A striking example of such a tactic may be found in the prominence which Hanoi accorded the deaths of detainees in the Phu-Loi prison camp in December 1958. Yet propaganda support and actual association with the insurrection at this stage were two different things. For the North there were a number of important reasons why the time was not opportune to become a major party in the insurgency. At a period when the role of Moscow as the leader of the Communist countries was much clearer, the policy of avoiding overt struggle in the pursuit of revolutionary aims was in the ascendant. More important, possibly, was the Hanoi politburo's need to evaluate its policies in terms of the strength of its state apparatus to meet a major challenge such as it would face if the United States should demonstrate its support for President Diem in a more dramatic military manner. The mistakes of the land reform period were only a few years old. And despite the admission of mistakes the Hanoi Government could not afford to embark upon policies which strained its population's capacities beyond reason.

Against such a background of a need to move with caution and to balance political advantage and military danger the Hanoi Government's claim not to have been implicated in the development of the insurgency should not be dismissed as lacking all basis and significance. The guerrilla insurgency which grew to increasingly serious proportions in 1959 and 1960 had clear southern roots, whatever the truth of claims and counter-claims about its direction. The former Viet-Minh cadres whose experience was vital to the rapid increase in guerrilla activity were predominantly men who had been born in southern Viet-Nam. There is some notable evidence, moreover, to suggest that the southern insurgency was an embarrassment to Hanoi, which saw in Diem's rule the seeds of his regime's own destruction. In a war situation where propaganda had played an extremely important part, the way in which assessments should be made of material beamed over clandestine radio stations is sometimes open to considerable debate. It is impossible, however, to dismiss the consistent evidence that Hanoi was, through broadcasts beamed to the south, indicating considerable reserve about the policies which the insurgents were following and the extent to which the insurgents had ignored the necessary ideological conditions which were essential for the successful conclusion of an armed rising.

If the debate cannot be satisfactorily resolved on the basis of the evidence which is available, there is little difficulty in briefly summarizing the situation in Viet-Nam at the beginning of the 1960s, at the time when the North Vietnamese Government finally placed its formal support behind the National Liberation Front. After more than six years of personal rule, President Diem, relying heavily upon the advice of his brother Nhu, had not been successful in giving any unity to his state. Repression directed against any who questioned his policies had brought an armed response from the countryside which was led by former Viet-Minh cadres, but which appealed, also, to a wide variety of persons who had no identification with Communism. In the cities Diem's policies had not rallied the intellectuals to his side. Some had joined the insurgents in the countryside. Others had refused to join forces with the armed opposition, but had made clear their opposition, most notably through the Caravelle Manifesto, a statement signed by eighteen influential Saigon residents, outlining grievances and giving a general critique of Diem's policies. Whatever its initial hesitations, the government of North Viet-Nam had come to give its firm support to the insurgents who fought the Diem regime's forces in the countryside.

But at this stage, no matter how closely Hanoi may have controlled overall policy, the base upon which the Liberation Front built was a southern one. The number of men who infiltrated into the south from North Viet-Nam was extremely small, and remained so until the period of major escalation in 1965. The supply of arms and equipment was, on occasion, important, but by far the greatest number of arms used by those who opposed the Diem government were captured from the South Vietnamese armed forces.

Increasingly introspective and more than ever unwilling to listen to advice, Ngo Dinh Diem and the government he led survived through the support of the military and through the economic contributions of the United States. That even the support of the military was suspect had been shown by the *coup manqué* mounted against the President by sections of the Army in November 1960. Diem's power base was shrinking. Insecurity in the countryside was leading to increasingly large areas passing out of government control. The only persons who could be considered truly loyal to the regime were the Catholics who had come south from North Viet-Nam in the 1954 and 1955 period and those conservatively oriented officials and administrators who saw their own fortunes linked with Diem's and accepted that his was a personal governance which would brook no criticism.

Many points could be chosen along the course of recent Vietnamese history as representing the critical point at which the United States became so deeply engaged in the affairs of the country that an easy withdrawal became impossible. Some observers have suggested that this point came as early as 1955 when President Eisenhower pledged support to Diem. Others would emphasize the period stretching from late 1964 (the time of the so-called Tonkin Gulf Incident) to the decision to commit large-scale American combat forces in 1965. The period from the beginning of 1961 until President Diem's death in 1963 has its own qualifications for being regarded as a particularly significant time in bringing about a situation in which the United States had committed so much of its national prestige to ensuring the survival of an anti-Communist South Viet-Nam as to make any withdrawal extremely difficult. It was a period, as one commentator observed, which led to the point in 1964 when one could say that there were no longer any good solutions for the United States in Viet-Nam.

Part of the significance of the 1961–3 period lies in the way that American officials either refused or were unable to perceive the nature of the challenge which was being posed to the Diem government. Insistence on the part of American officials and military men that the insurgency in the countryside was essentially an externally inspired affair led to their accepting with surprisingly little critical analysis the accounts of developments which Diem and his advisers gave of the progress of efforts to counter the guerrilla war. Nowhere is this to be seen more dramatically than in the case of the Strategic Hamlet Program. This programme for the resettlement and regroupment of the South Vietnamese rural population came to be the Diem regime's chief strategy against the rural insurrection. At the same time it was accepted by senior American officials, both military and civilian, as a guarantee both of the serious commitment of Diem's government to winning the war and of the possibility of achieving that aim. What these officials failed to recognize was that the programme was, from the very beginning, of dubious relevance to the South Vietnamese situation. And even if the concept had been right, the way in which the plan was implemented would have prevented it from ever playing a conclusive part in undermining the insurgency which gripped the rural regions of South Viet-Nam.

Faced with the growth of rural insecurity, and recognizing the extent to which a failure to exert control over the villages in the rural regions aided the insurgents, a decision was taken in 1961 to develop a Strategic Hamlet Program. Some efforts had been made before that date to isolate the peasants of South Viet-Nam from the insurgents through resettlement. The Agroville Scheme had been the most ambitious of these attempts. Under this scheme the South Vietnamese Government had planned to resettle some three hundred thousand peasants away from their traditional villages, free from contact with the guerrilla insurgents, over a period of some four years. Instituted in 1959, the scheme, with rare exceptions, was a failure. It was apparent that the government had not fully considered the implications of resettlement on such a scale. The peasants showed themselves to be highly resistant to moves to transfer them from their ancestral lands. Those who did move under government direction found that the areas to which they had been sent were frequently highly unsatisfactory for farming. Relocated on bare ground which lacked the shade trees which went with their original homes, the Vietnamese peasants then had to contend with the fact that the promised aid for building a new dwelling was either insufficient or lacking altogether. The peasants were called on to perform forced labour on public works, such as canals, and in one well-documented instance they found that when they had been resettled their ricefields were six transportless miles away from their settlement.

The generally unsatisfactory character of the Agroville Scheme further harmed the Diem regime's position. It left peasants discontented and played into the hands of the insurgents who were able to capitalize on the scheme's mistakes for propaganda purposes as they sought to gain further recruits and to convince the wavering of the short-comings of the existing government. The scheme was also a focus of criticism for the non-Communist urban opposition. The mistakes of the plan and its implementation formed part of the Caravelle group's critique of Diem and his rule where emphasis was placed both on the undesirability of forced resettlement and on the extent to which the insurgents were profiting from the many mistakes and errors that had been made.

It was while official South Vietnamese press reports continued to extol the questionable benefits of the Agroville Scheme that, in July 1961, the first references appeared to a new resettlement concept, the Strategic Hamlet Program. The genesis of the programme has never been clearly established in published accounts of its development. President Diem's brother, Ngo Dinh Nhu, was to claim the credit for the programme at the time when the concept was seen as certain to save South Viet-Nam from Communism. Some have suggested that American officials were the first to propose the virtues of a nation-wide resettlement programme, being by this stage aware of the extent to which resettlement in new villages had been important in the resolutions of the Malayan Emergency. Finally, the influence of British advisers, led by Brigadier Thompson (later Sir Robert Thompson), in introducing the strategic hamlet policy was of considerable importance, though the evidence available does not suggest that the original decision stemmed from British advice.

The uncertainty about exactly how the decision to develop strategic hamlets was reached is matched by the doubt over the precise date of the actual implementation of the plan. References appeared in the Vietnamese news bulletins to strategic hamlets being constructed in July 1961; but the governmental committee established to control the programme did not come into being until some seven months later. Some well-informed commentators would choose March 1962 as the starting date for the programme. It was then that the most ambitious of any of the strategic hamlet operations, under the code name 'Operation Sunrise', began in an area just to the north of Saigon.

Not only was Operation Sunrise ambitious, it provides an illustration of the difficulties inherent in the entire programme. The peasants who had been selected for re-settlement were reluctant to move. In part this was because of the counter-pressures placed upon them by the strongly entrenched insurgent forces in the region. In part the reluctance was the result of a deep attachment to their land which, for the Vietnamese, involves such strong personal ties as the need to care for the graves of one's fore-bears. Faced with this reluctance, coercion was necessary if the government forces were to achieve their aims. The houses which the peasants vacated were burned, and in some cases no compensation was offered for the property destroyed. The new hamlets in which the peasants were then resettled were found to have little protection, and in one notable instance no way of communicating with the South Vietnamese armed forces, in the case of an attack by the insurgents, other than by runner.

The harsh measures adopted were defended in terms of the British experience in Malaya during the Emergency. Then, it is true, firm action was taken on occasion. But those who justified the firm action taken in South Viet-Nam, as the Strategic Hamlet Program got under way, seem to have failed to appreciate the way in which, in the Malayan experience, the government was meticulous in providing compensation. And, more important than compensation, the Malayan Government acted firmly but successfully. Resettled squatters were protected from Chinese guerrilla insurgents. Social services which were promised did materialize. In short, and at the most basic level, one of the great contrasts between the measures adopted in Malaya and those which were attempted in Viet-Nam was in the level of efficiency. Whatever the major myths which dominated American thinking on the options which could be pursued in Viet-Nam, the distorting effect of misplaced belief in the genuine commitment of their Asian ally to the same goals and the same level of efficiency has been one of the constant problems.

The example of Malaya, and the success which the British achieved there did much to bedevil rational analysis of the situation in Viet-Nam. How it should have been that the presumed similarities between Malaya in the 1940s and 1950s and Viet-Nam in the 1960s outweighed the need to recognize the profound *differences* between the two regions must remain one of the most puzzling aspects of the whole series of mistakes associated with the Strategic Hamlet Program.

From a military point of view there were indeed some similarities. In both regions an established government faced a Communist-led guerrilla challenge to its authority; and both in Malaya and in South Viet-Nam there were good reasons for believing that part of the answer to containing the guerrilla challenge lay in isolating the insurgents in the countryside from the uncommitted, or uncertainly committed, peasantry. However, when due account is taken of these essentially superficial similarities, the differences between the situations in Malaya and Viet-Nam remain profound. The insurgency in Viet-Nam was not mounted by an ethnically separate group which was easily identifiable, as was the case of the Chinese in Malaya. Whereas the Chinese in Malaya could provide very little proof of their claim to be the leaders of a national challenge to the British colonial administration, the insurgents in South Viet-Nam could claim to be in a direct line of descent from those men who had successfully brought the departure of the French after nearly one hundred years of colonial rule. And there was another, and strangely ironic contrast between the colonial situation of the Malayan Emergency and the non-colonial situation of Viet-Nam. In Malaya when disagreeable decisions had to be taken the blame could always be placed on the colonial authorities. In South Viet-Nam no such opportunity existed. South Vietnamese decisions, however much they might be presented by Communist propaganda as the result of American dictation, were identified with the South Vietnamese Government. The dual results of this situation were that Diem's government could not escape responsibility for its mistakes and, at the same time, that there was a tendency to avoid those decisions which seemed likely to cause difficulty for an individual South Vietnamese official.

But over and beyond the clear differences which can be shown to have existed between Malaya and Viet-Nam when the strategy of resettlement was adopted, was the apparent failure of those who supported the Strategic Hamlet Program to recognize the extent to which in Viet-Nam the pre-1954 past could not be wiped out. Not only did the quantitative differences between the scale of the insurgency in Malaya and Viet-Nam mean that plans which had worked in Malaya were less certain of success in another setting. Just as importantly, the background of the First Indochinese War had left a legacy of security problems in the countryside which the Hamlet Program could not overcome. Those who still believe that the Strategic Hamlet Program could have worked must base their counter-factual arguments on the premise that greater planning and slower and more careful implementation would have brought a very different result. Yet even if there had been these technical differences, the difficulty remains that at no time during the Diem regime did it seem likely that the government could muster sufficient devotion and expertise to match the hopes of those foreigners who, whatever their dedication, could not provide in themselves the commitment and devotion to a vision of the future which was to be found on the Communist but not on the anti-Communist side.

With the inexorable progress of tragedy, the Strategic Hamlet Program in the final year of President Diem's government became more and more over-extended with resultant gains for the insurgents. Yet while this was happening both South Vietnamese and American spokesmen lauded its development. The true state of affairs, in contrast, was one in which government control over the countryside was steadily eroded. Diem and his brother might claim that within the programme an opportunity was being provided for the extension of the curious philosophy of 'Personalism', but this was the rationalization of the leaders of a regime who themselves were behaving in a less than rational manner. As for the approving comments of United States officials, there seems no way of escaping the conclusion that such highly placed men as Secretary of Defence McNamara and General Earle Wheeler had become the victims of biased reporting of events, in which hopes for success were accorded more importance than the need for a rigorous examination of the true state of security in the countryside.

The hollowness of the whole fabric of misplaced hopes which had grown up around the Strategic Hamlet Program was revealed in the chaotic months which followed the overthrow of Ngo Dinh Diem's government in November 1963. The supposed gains which had come from the programme were found in most cases to be gains on paper, not in fact. Rural security after nearly ten years of authoritarian rule was in a parlous state for the Saigon Government. The deceptions and delusions of Diemist rule had left the insurgents closer to, not more distant from, gaining power over the south.

Yet, close though they were to power, the insurgents could not achieve their goal of a general uprising which would sweep the successive United States-backed regimes in Saigon from office. Dominating large areas of the countryside and a large proportion of the rural population, the insurgents had still not succeeded in gaining a sufficiently large base in the urban concentrations to provide the necessary conditions for an effective rising. In this situation the strategy of the insurgents changed. Abandoning the slower policy of a guerrilla campaign aimed at the eventual emergence of a successful general uprising, they now increasingly pursued a policy of major military confrontation with the weakened Saigon forces. Students of the shifts and tensions within the Hanoi politburo see in the changed strategy a victory for the policies of General Vo Nguyen Giap over his more theoretically oriented colleague and rival for power, Truong Chinh. If such a judgement is correct, there is nevertheless no reason to believe that Giap's success in promoting his policy implied any belief that eventual victory would be either quick or easy. The experience of the First Indochinese War has always been with the men who have directed the fortunes of those fighting against Saigon and the United States in the Second War.

In the closing months of 1964, with the capacity of the South Vietnamese Army declining more and more sharply, there seemed every reason for the insurgents to believe that major changes in their favour were in sight. These might not have represented total victory, for an American readiness to give up its support for the Saigon regime was scarcely to be expected. By this stage there were North Vietnamese troops operating in the South, but even if one relies upon official United States estimates the five thousand involved were fewer than the United States advisers, and the amount of war material which the Hanoi Government was sending south was small in comparison with the massive military supplies which flowed in from America. In this situation the American decision (apparently reached by President Johnson *before* the 1964 American presidential election was held) to seek an end to the Viet-Nam conflict through a massive commitment of American combat troops was taken. The decision transformed the war from a guerrilla struggle and changed its character from what had been essentially a civil conflict into a major international confrontation. When American combat troops became engaged in Viet-Nam in large numbers North Viet-Nam saw its interests as so vitally threatened that it committed substantial numbers of regular forces in response.

From 1965 onwards Viet-Nam sustained the experience

of war on a much more massive scale than anything it had known before. The extension of aerial bombardment to the section of the country north of the seventeenth parallel was matched by a greatly increased programme of bombing in the south. The planned and unplanned devastation of large regions of South Viet-Nam which were considered to be in the hands of the insurgents led to the dramatic growth of a refugee problem of tragic dimensions. In the expectation that continuous pressure on the enemy would lead him to sue for peace, the United States high command in Saigon embarked on aggressive search and destroy operations, designed to inflict such casualties that the opposing forces would no longer have the will to fight. In the face of previous failures to compete successfully with the insurgents for control of the peasantry, a new attempt was made to extend pacification effects which would ensure that security and social services did reach the villagers.

In the face of this phenomenal effort on so many fronts the failure of the United States to reach a successful military conclusion to the war demands explanation. The easy answer which has been chosen by General Westmoreland, the former commander of American forces in Viet-Nam and the current Chief of Staff of the United States Army, is that political limitations set upon the activities of his forces hindered them from attaining a victory which was not impossible. Ghostly echoes of the claim that the First Indochinese War was lost in Paris hang about this estimation. While in one sense it is beyond argument that the United States did not commit the maximum force in the pursuit of its aims in Viet-Nam, it is also beyond dispute that in any modern war the limitations of political considerations, mostly domestic considerations, cannot be ignored. Much more to the point in any effort to understand why the United States should have been stalemated in Viet-Nam is an attempt to discover where American estimations of the nature of the conflict were inaccurate.

The history of United States bombing of North Viet-

Nam provides an insight into the mis-estimations which were made. The first aerial strikes north of the seventeenth parallel, in August of 1964, were designed as a warning to North Viet-Nam of the high cost which would be exacted if it did not heed Washington's warnings to cease its activities in the south. The sustained raids which began in February of 1965 were mounted in the belief that the government and people of North Viet-Nam would come to recognize that the experience of daily bombing was too high a price to pay. The emphasis frequently given in official bulletins to the way in which the bombing of North Viet-Nam was designed to boost morale in the south need not be entirely discounted, but the chief aim of the bombardment was to hasten the North Vietnamese capitulation.

Such an aim was not achieved, since the North Vietnamese – just as was the case with the civilian population of both Britain and Germany during the Second World War – instead of buckling under pressure were spurred to greater efforts. Quite in contrast to the expectations of American planners, the effect of sustained bombing was a stiffening of national will. Moreover, the bombing neither succeeded in stemming the flow of North Vietnamese troops and supplies to the south, nor led to any indication that the Hanoi regime would abandon its interests in the south.

The view that the bombing would bring radical change in the attitude held in Hanoi is related directly to the fundamental myth which has postulated the continued existence of two separate states in Viet-Nam. The north was expected to give way just because planners on the American side failed to recognize how deeply Hanoi's interests were engaged in the conflict. Insistence upon the concept of Hanoi's interest in South Viet-Nam being 'aggression' hindered appreciation of the deep commitment which Hanoi had to the reunification of the country. While it is possible that the application of greater American force both in the south and through aerial bombardment of the north might have discouraged the Hanoi Government from further fighting, there is no satisfactory way of estimating at what point such a development might have occurred. Hanoi and sections of Haiphong were spared from the worst effects of bombing, but there is sufficient evidence from non-Communist as well as Communist sources to show that the bombardment of North Viet-Nam was carried on to the point where few militarily important targets were left unscathed.

In assessing developments in South Viet-Nam, the same failure to take account of the motivations and commitment of the insurgents to their goals seems to have affected American military thinking. An obsession with organizational theory has led to analysis of Viet-Cong activity which has made the technical aspects of guerrilla operations and political endeavour seem more important than the ideals which inspire that activity. It would be necessary to grasp at some of the least convincing myths accepted by critics of American involvement in the Viet-Nam War in order to imagine that all who fight against the forces of Saigon and the United States do so from a pure belief in the virtue of their cause. There has undoubtedly been coercion and indoctrination to convince so many young men and women that they should risk possible death in actions against the enemy. Yet to dismiss the success of the insurgents as the result merely of supreme organizational ability is to suggest that only on one side can the importance of ideals have a place. Such an assertion is a crude and arrogant, and even racialist, view of the nature of the war. It is a view which has been reinforced as the result of the frustration which so many American official spokesmen have felt at the obvious evidence that energy and determination have so often appeared to be more evident among the enemy than America's client government.

In many ways the myths of the left have been a mirror image of the view which has refused to see the importance of ideals to the insurgent forces in South Viet-Nam. For the impassioned critics of the United States position there has been as much reluctance to examine in detail the facts and subtleties of the Vietnamese scene as has been present among the supporters of American policy. Most notably, the non-Communist critics of United States involvement have repeatedly shied away from recognizing the force and importance of Communist thought in the Vietnamese revolution. Criticism has correctly pointed to the faults and fallacies of American planning, but failed to accept the extent to which the overthrow of the Saigon regime by the insurgents is likely to lead to the ultimate success of Communist-led forces. There has been, instead, a search to find a 'third force'. At one stage the Buddhists seemed ready to fit this role. At other times the non-Communist members of the insurgent leadership were judged as able to play a much stronger role than evidence has ever suggested was likely.

Although it is possible to develop some important arguments to suggest that an earlier settlement to the war which pre-dated the period of escalation and so of increased bitterness might have had a moderating influence on insurgent policy, there has been little reason to think, since 1965, that any third force would wield much power. Too much blood has been spilt and too much bitterness has developed for the Hanoi Government and those who follow its policies in the south to accept any other goal than their right to control the country as a whole. Whatever transition period might be settled upon, if they indeed are successful in their search for power, their ultimate aims seem clear and unequivocal. And with such aims of total control the possibility of a bloodbath cannot easily be dismissed. The dimensions of the retribution likely to be visited upon those identified as enemies of the state cannot be accurately predicted. It may well be that it could be smaller than many have calculated, just because of the remaining civil war characteristics of the Vietnamese situation. Nonetheless, it would be foolish to pretend that the risk of bloody retribution does not exist.

The most important single factor in exploding the myths

which have been associated with Viet-Nam, no matter what side they have come from, was the sustained offensive which was launched by the insurgents and the North Vietnamese troops in South Viet-Nam during Tet (January-February) 1968. The importance of this offensive did not lie in the question of whether or not the offensive brought the anti-Saigon forces a military victory, however such a victory is to be judged. The impact and the significance of the offensive lay in the manner in which, for the first time, the United States and its allies were forced to reassess the assumptions which lay beneath their policy. If the ultimate results of this assessment remain uncertain in early 1971, the immediate significance is already fairly clearly established. Following the Tet offensive the United States abandoned its belief in the possibility of winning a clear military victory in South Viet-Nam. Despite the hesitations which have hung about United States policy from the end of March 1968 and the apparent assumption of a more militant position shown in the extension of operations to Cambodia and Laos, there has been continuing evidence that American officials now recognize that a future settlement in Viet-Nam may have to provide a place for the National Liberation Front.

There are many ways in which such a development may be considered. There will always be an important number of commentators who, as steadfast supporters of the initial American decision to intervene in Viet-Nam, will argue that military victory could have been achieved and that more time, more men and more patience could have brought the desired goal. There will be critics who will insist on the success of the insurgents in reaching their goal through a greater degree of bravery and rectitude than was shown by their enemy. The best analyses will be less partisan, even if in seeking to eschew the excesses of either ideologically-oriented position they prove less emotionally satisfying.

Fighting within the existing situation, and not within some ideal in which all the factors of importance could be controlled, the southern insurgents and the North Vietnamese forces under Vo Nguyen Giap's control succeeded in imposing a military stalemate. Such a stalemate is not, in itself, success, but from the point of view of those who have fought against Saigon, a stalemate represents the first condition for later success. The number of troops who have lost their lives on the North Vietnamese and insurgent sides is horrifying for a Western observer to contemplate. But this reaction should never have hidden the fact that General Giap and his fellow military and political leaders were prepared to accept such staggering losses.

In terms of political developments within South Viet-Nam, reassessments which have followed upon the Tet offensive have brought the conclusion that, whatever the Saigon leadership's determination to survive, and whatever the measure of success achieved through the 'Vietnamization' programme, there still has to be convincing evidence that South Viet-Nam's military-backed leadership is committed to a policy which has the possibility of real success in rallying the population behind it. The formation of mass fronts for national unity has sounded attractive from the point of view of propaganda, but the actual political results of such endeavours have been remarkably small. The constant problem which has beset the Saigon Government has been the fact that its political and military opponent, the National Liberation Front, represents the strongest and most developed political force in South Viet-Nam. The results of elections – which specifically excluded Communist and neutralist candidates from participation – have been quoted to show that the existing Saigon leadership has an electorally-backed claim to power. But in a region which has little understanding of an electoral process and with only an election in which not all could participate to cite as evidence, the firm reality of Liberation Front power must be recognized. Whatever the strength of the South Vietnamese Army, and the capacity of the Saigon leadership to bring voters to the poll, there is still no evidence of any other political body in

South Viet-Nam which can match the dedication and the organization of the Front. The National Liberation Front has not been destroyed. It shows no inclination to abandon its basic aims. And short of either its destruction, which now seems extremely unlikely, or its self-imposed dissolution, which seems impossible, it must be considered and given some important place in a future settlement.

In the countryside the effects of the Tet offensive were such as to bring a questioning of the efficacy of the pacification programme which had been undertaken and lauded over the preceding two years. Despite the recoveries which Saigon claims to have made since 1968, there is no firm evidence that the Front's infrastructure, its highly skilled and clandestine organizational apparatus, has been eliminated from the villages. The number of villagers who are reported under the control of the Saigon Government has steadily risen, but little emphasis is given in official news releases to the fact that the bulk of those who are said to be under Saigon's 'control' live in hamlets where there are continuing major difficulties in ensuring and maintaining security. Indeed, the necessity of achieving government control in the rural regions may well have been met more through the intensive bombing raids which have taken place in South Viet-Nam, forcing vast numbers of peasants to become urban refugees, than through the efforts of 'Revolutionary Development' pacification teams. Whatever might be the true state of rural security and the degree of control which the Saigon regime exercises in the provincial regions, the experience of Tet 1968 has left permanent doubt about the possibility of any pacification programme achieving rapid results and so a dramatic change in the nature of the war and of the terms under which it could be concluded. With more time the result might have been different, but 'more time' might have been a decade or longer.

No commentator can appraise the war in Viet-Nam in any final sense until a permanent agreement to end hostilities has been achieved. But the absence of such an agreement in early 1971 does not prevent commentary on the nature of the war and its causes.

The emphasis in this chapter has been on the extent to which myths came to dominate thinking on Viet-Nam, and on the extent to which less than rigorous standards of analysis were adopted by those who chose to support the positions adopted by successive regimes in Saigon. Yet in a consideration of the overall problem of political developments in Southeast Asia, there is another way to look at events in Viet-Nam. Consideration may be given to the extent to which Viet-Nam, and the war which has been waged there, represents a special case because of the involvement of Communists in the efforts to subvert the government of South Viet-Nam. Was, and is, the war in Viet-Nam qualitatively different because its pattern has been dictated by men who have a political allegiance to Communism?

At one level the answer to such a question must be in the affirmative. There seems little doubt that the organizational capacities of the Communist-led forces in Viet-Nam must be judged to stem, to some extent, from the particular talents which Communist parties have demonstrated in Southeast Asia for administrative and political organization. In contrast to so many other political groups, the Communists in Viet-Nam have shown that they are both dedicated and capable. On the one hand, if there had been other non-Communist organizations in Viet-Nam with the same capacity and dedication, the history of Viet-Nam might have been very different. But, on the other hand, to place too great an emphasis on organization risks ignoring the very real extent to which the war in Viet-Nam has been fought for goals which are easily recognized as common to much of the armed conflict which has been part of the history of Southeast Asia. Despite the transformation which took place in the Viet-Nam War once the United States became engaged on a major scale, the conflict did, and still does, have elements of a civil war character to it – the revolt of one section of the same nation against another. And, just because of the American involvement, another feature of the war has remained which in other circumstances might have disappeared. In the First Indochinese War, irrespective of the Communist leadership which directed the battle against the French, the conflict represented an anti-colonial effort of a large section of a nation against alien overlords. In a very real sense the same element has remained in the Second Indochinese War, only in this case the alien power has ceased to be France and become America.

To view the war in Viet-Nam in terms which give excessive force to the fact that the revolt has been led by Communists is to make two major errors. First, there is the error which assumes that Communism can create revolt without the existence of genuine grievances which will seek some answer, no matter which political philosophy finally provides it. Secondly, there is the error which has so consistently been present throughout the long and bitter discussion of developments in Viet-Nam. This error has involved the failure to see that Communism and nationalism in Viet-Nam can be one and the same thing. The inability of many political leaders to appreciate this fact has brought a tragic harvest of death and destruction to perhaps the most sorely tried of the countries of Southeast Asia.

# Chapter 9

# Toppling the God-King

The challenge mounted against the Saigon regime has been led by men dedicated to left-wing ideals. In marked contrast, the overthrow of Prince Sihanouk in Cambodia was engineered by men who are politically to the right of centre. One consequence of their action, taken in March 1970, has been a widening of the Viet-Nam War. Yet while this dramatic development was of profound international significance, Sihanouk's deposition is best understood in terms of a classic instance of revolt; a revolt stemming directly from elite rivalry. The immediate military consequence in South Viet-Nam of the *coup d'état* and the American and South Vietnamese intervention in Cambodia was a period of diminished military activity following the temporary destruction, in mid 1970, of Vietnamese Communist sanctuaries across the border. In Cambodia itself, however, the Allied intervention brought a military response from the Vietnamese Communists and pro-Sihanouk Cambodian forces which by the end of 1970 left large areas of the country outside the control of the Phnom Penh Government.

Indeed, when the military situation is considered, the public optimism which the Phnom Penh leadership was displaying at the end of 1970 seems difficult to explain. Yet optimism, even euphoria, were the dominant tones in political life in Phnom Penh. Having deposed Prince Sihanouk, General Lon Nol and former Prince Sirik Matak pursued policies which, if sometimes puzzling to external observers, appeared to receive the enthusiastic support of the urban-based elite in Phnom Penh. Diplomatic relations were restored with Thailand and South Viet-Nam. Sihanouk's policy of guarded tolerance of the Vietnamese

Communists of both North and South Viet-Nam was replaced by an overt policy of opposition to Hanoi and the National Liberation Front so long as these continued to maintain forces on Cambodian soil. The tentative efforts at *rapprochement* which Sihanouk had pursued in relation to the United States were replaced by a full-scale attempt to involve the U.S. Government in Cambodia's battles.

The transformation of the internal situation was no less dramatic. For years the conventional wisdom in commentary on Cambodian affairs argued that Prince Sihanouk represented the only form of leadership likely to unite a state which, for the most part, was ethnically homogeneous but economically and politically backward. The best-known popular image of Sihanouk was that contained in the photographs which showed him surrounded by Cambodian peasants, receiving the homage of those who still thought of him as a king but encouraging them to join him in transforming Cambodia into a modern state. To a degree the iconography of these photographs was valid. The Prince was held in awe by the peasantry and on his provincial tours he constantly urged upon them the value of modern agriculture and education. But as with any icon, the photographs could only show one aspect of Cambodian life, and there were other, less reassuring, realities which the Ministry of Information material disguised. The inadequacy of such images is shown by the fact that only a little more than six months after Sihanouk's deposition the institution of monarchy, with all the symbolic trappings of unity supposedly enshrined within it, was abolished. Royal titles have gone, as have, at least in theory, the special privileges attached to birth into the large, factious but frequently wealthy families with former royal connections.

Many uncertainties attach to any analysis of very recent developments in Cambodia, but it is possible to give at least a coherent account of what led to the toppling of the Cambodian god-king – for such Sihanouk remained for a long time, despite his abdication from the throne in 1955.

Throughout the late 1950s and for much of the 1960s foreign commentators on Cambodia were bemused by the dazzling personality of Prince Sihanouk and anxious to see in him an exemplar of enlightened, socially conscious and non-Communist leadership. They tended then to ignore the realities of Cambodia. To a considerable extent the adulation which Sihanouk received from observers in Western countries hinged on the fact that he was able, over some fifteen years, to save his country from the ravages of war afflicting the neighbouring states of Viet-Nam and Laos. This proposition cannot be denied and events since Sihanouk's deposition have certainly provided a marked and tragic contrast with the previous situation. But there is a paradox involved; Prince Sihanouk managed to preserve a fragile peace in his country only by permitting substantial numbers of North Vietnamese and National Liberation Front troops to occupy base and supply positions on Cambodian soil. In the baldest terms, peace was preserved in Cambodia through the pursuit of a policy which led to the disappearance of Cambodian control over large areas of the country – particularly in the northeast, and to a lesser degree in the southeast – and that policy became a catalyst in producing the decision to depose Sihanouk.

Future historians are likely to argue over the question of whether Prince Sihanouk could have acted other than as he did in relation to the Vietnamese Communists' use of Cambodian territory. It remains true that he did pursue a policy which permitted the progressively increasing use of his country's territory by an ever-growing number of anti-Saigon troops. But the extent to which Sihanouk, in following this policy, should best be seen as a victim of greater forces over which he had no control is a matter for real debate. Events in Cambodia over the past decade have been closely linked with developments in Viet-Nam. By the middle 1960s there was considerable evidence that Prince Sihanouk had come to the conclusion that the

L

likely winners in the struggle taking place in Viet-Nam would be the Hanoi Government and the southern National Liberation Front. It was in these circumstances that the Prince first gave some measure of approval for Vietnamese Communist troops to use Cambodian territory.

The nature of this approval and the limits set upon the Vietnamese troops' activities are not known with any precision. The new regime in Phnom Penh has presented an account of Prince Sihanouk's dealings with the Vietnamese Communists which is so insistent in its allegations of Sihanouk's almost total subservience to the Vietnamese as to be open to severe question. Nevertheless, whatever the nature of the arrangements clandestinely concluded in the middle 1960s, by 1969 the situation had been very considerably transformed: in the earlier period the number of Vietnamese Communist troops in Cambodia at any one time was limited, but by the end of 1969 there were fifty thousand soldiers in the country.

The massive use of aerial bombardment and ground firepower in South Viet-Nam by the American and South Vietnamese forces enormously increased the importance of the Cambodian sanctuaries. And Cambodia additionally provided the route through which substantial supplies of *matériel* were moved to the insurgent forces in South Viet-Nam itself. Willingly or otherwise, Sihanouk's policies had led to a situation in which Cambodia had become vitally important to the war effort of the Communists.

The dangers of Cambodia's position had certainly not escaped him. But the efforts which he was making in 1969 to ameliorate the situation fell far short of success. A limited political *rapprochement* with the United States was related to his readiness to permit some instances of hot pursuit of retreating North Vietnamese and National Liberation Front forces by American and South Vietnamese troops across Cambodia's borders. The small Cambodian army was, by December 1969, heavily engaged in attempts to contain the presence of Vietnamese Communist forces in the northeast provinces of Ratnakiri and Mondolkiri. These attempts had, however, done little more than attract the attention of the Cambodian urban-based elite to the situation which existed within the country's borders. When Sihanouk departed for medical treatment in France in early January 1970 those left in charge of government, and the politically active and interested population within the capital, looked with increasing concern at what they believed to be the virtual occupation of areas of their country by an alien force which no longer showed any concern for Cambodian susceptibilities.

The unwanted presence of the North Vietnamese and National Liberation Front troops was crucial to the final decision to confront and then depose Sihanouk, but it seems best judged as having been the catalyst which worked upon a waiting range of other, deeply felt grievances. Moreover, it is fundamentally important to recognize that it was the feeling of grievance among the urban-based elite rather than among the peasantry which was instrumental in bringing Sihanouk's overthrow. Such a contention does not accord well with the popularly held picture of Sihanouk's most important base of support being the peasants. Yet while there need be no doubt that Sihanouk was viewed in semi-divine terms by the peasantry, their support for his position was essentially passive and reactive.

This has, historically, always been the case in Cambodia. Against this, support from the urban elite in both historical and contemporary times has had to be positive if the regime was to survive. For the urban-based elite – both those who served in the capital itself and those, pre-eminently members of the army officer corps, who served away from Phnom Penh but saw their interests linked with capital politics – have always been the men who had access to power.

The extent of residual support for the Prince among the peasantry will be one of the most important determinants in the success or failure of the attempts by those opposing the new regime to rouse the peasants' support by appealing to their loyalty to Sihanouk. That Sihanouk was viewed in semi-divine terms in the past might not be any guarantee that this is how he is regarded now that he is no longer in power.

The underlying sense of discontent felt by the urban-based elite by 1970 was related to three major questions. There was first a sense of frustration at the results of Prince Sihanouk's economic policies, which had struck at what had once been well-assured opportunities for financial gain. A second major concern was the belief that Prince Sihanouk's consort, Madame Monique, was seeking to gain not only financially but also politically from her position. And finally, there was a growing conviction that Prince Sihanouk himself was no longer ready to devote himself to the duties of the state with the necessary energies those duties required.

The decisions which Prince Sihanouk took in 1963 and 1964 to nationalize the economy and introduce a policy of austerity threatened the economic interests of the elite. Initially the measures reduced Cambodia's foreign exchange debt. But two more long-term effects followed. First, it became apparent that the result of the new measures was a sharp falling-off in business activity. Far from merely affecting the foreign community, as Sihanouk apparently expected, this decline had considerable effect on Cambodians as well. Secondly, areas of the economy not immediately connected with commercial endeavour declined concurrently. Not least, the general level of return from what is loosely termed corruption fell significantly.

The deprivations suffered by the richer members of the Cambodian elite were fairly obvious. But because of what might be called the 'filtration effect' of corruption in Cambodia the austerity measures introduced by Sihanouk were bound to affect the incomes of a whole range of civil servants. The substantial rewards gained by senior officials in the course of approving particular transactions were not

matched at lower administrative levels. But they had their
equivalents, even if these were not financial equivalents,
of the same magnitude. The point is that all levels in the
administrative machine, which is predominantly Cambodian in ethnic composition, benefited to some degree from
the manner in which the economic mechanism operated
before 1963. And all levels suffered in the period of austerity. Prince Sihanouk spoke only too truly when he observed in July 1966 that he '. . . *did not care a rap about
political economy*'.

One notably important group found their professional
and corporate interests in danger as the result of the austerity measures. This group was the Cambodian officer
corps. In a country in which there are few groups which
display both a feeling of *esprit de corps* and a sense of
national purpose, these characteristics are to be found in
the army. Well before 1970, there were pressures within
the army to seek a change in Sihanouk's policies. The end
of American aid to Cambodia in 1963 led the army to a
desperate search for supplies from France, China and the
Soviet Union. The result was an ill-assorted inventory of
weaponry. Even more dramatically, there were occasions
when the army was unable to carry out its duties along
Cambodia's borders because of a shortage of fuel for its
vehicles. Dissident feeling within the army stemming from
Sihanouk's immediate policies was strengthened by the
nostalgia of some senior officers for the perquisites of office
which had been available in the period of American aid.
Prince Sihanouk was at least partly correct when he observed in January 1968 that the army was pro-American
in its sympathies. The signal irony of the situation was
that it was the new Prime Minister, General Lon Nol, who
played a major part at the time in restraining his officers
from following a path of disloyalty to Sihanouk.

Against the background of a general feeling of depriva-
tion among members of the urban-based elite, Prince Sihanouk's consort, Madame Monique, emerged into view in
1968 as a woman devoted to personal aggrandizement on

a major scale. The benefits which had been gained before 1963 and 1964 by the urban elite as a whole might best be described as 'functional' corruption. In a country which pays its state employees totally inadequate salaries there should be little surprise that functional corruption is widespread. But from the middle of 1968 onwards it was widely believed in Phnom Penh that Monique's corrupt activities had gone beyond the accepted norm.

But whatever resentment was felt in relation to her pursuit of wealth and her efforts to advance the interests of her half-brother, Colonel Oum Mannorine, paled into insignificance beside the feeling aroused by the belief that she was, in the latter part of 1969, seeking to advance her own political interests and those of her son Prince Norodom Tokyo. Monique was, many members of the urban elite believed, seeking to persuade Sihanouk to reassume the throne which he renounced in 1955. Such a decision on his part would have given her much greater power and opened the way to her son's future accession, in place of Sihanouk's previously designated successor, Prince Norodom Naradipo.

The final major factor upon which the catalyst was to work involved the growing belief that Prince Sihanouk was no longer prepared to engage in the hard work of government. Casual students of Cambodian affairs will be surprised at such a suggestion, for the image promoted by Sihanouk's propaganda organization was of a man constantly at work on his country's behalf. Increasingly, however, from the middle onwards, this image was more apparent than real. Despite his constant public appearances, Sihanouk showed less and less inclination to deal with the immediate concerns of the state. His failure to deal with his country's economic problems had other parallels.

The earlier apparent success of his international policies was more and more in question as the war continued in Viet-Nam. The brilliant decision, taken in 1955, to institute a national political movement which would transcend the squabbles of party politics was less and less convincing as the movement itself, the People's Socialist Community, became more and more politicized. The great need which Cambodia had for an extension of educational facilities when it gained independence in 1953 did not require Prince Sihanouk's answer. This involved an excessive expansion of secondary and tertiary education, to the point where the high school and university graduates who had been pushed through the system had nowhere to turn for employment, despite their degrees and diplomas.

For many elite Cambodians, Prince Sihanouk's devotion to film-making epitomized his unreadiness to treat state business in a serious manner. Of an aesthetic quality praised only by those for whom pleasing Sihanouk was more important than the free exercise of artistic judgement, the Prince's films became a symbol of frivolity. Unready to delegate power, Prince Sihanouk delayed and postponed decision-making. By inhibiting his subordinates, who feared loss of position should they offend him, Sihanouk brought about a *malaise* in the Cambodian administration. One of the most significant ways in which this situation was revealed was in the unreadiness of men to act in Sihanouk's absence.

Until the entry into office of the Lon Nol-Sirik Matak government in August 1969, no official dared to act in the Prince's absence. When Sihanouk was in the country the pace of government was slow in the extreme. In the provinces a lack of real liaison between the centre and the outlying regions led either to the cessation of any significant government activity or to a readiness on the part of some more confident officials to act entirely in their own interests. The growing evidence since 1966 of regional disunity in Cambodia, and the growth of an insurgency movement with left-wing and Communist sympathies were, to a considerable extent, responses to this situation.

Against these background considerations and with deepening concern at the extent to which the Vietnamese Communists were using Cambodian territory.

Against these background considerations and with deepening concern at the extent to which the Vietnamese Communists were using Cambodian territory, Sihanouk's critics planned his overthrow. All available evidence indicates that the decision to depose Prince Sihanouk was essentially a Cambodian one, in terms of both planning and motivation. But there are some shadowy aspects to the affair which suggest that official United States and South Vietnamese knowledge of the plotters' intentions was probably greater than has so far been documented. This seems clear now that we know of the part played in the *coup's* planning by the long-time Cambodian dissident Son Ngoc Thanh, a bitter enemy of Sihanouk since before Cambodia achieved independence. Thanh with South Vietnamese and Thai – and in a less certain fashion United States – assistance had worked to bring down Sihanouk throughout the 1960s. His involvement in the plot makes it impossible to believe that the United States was totally unaware of developments. But to transform awareness into some allegation of external direction remains unjustified on the basis of available evidence. To attribute major responsibility for the planning and execution of the *coup* to others than Cambodians is a curiously ethnocentric judgement which ignores internal events in Cambodia over the past five years.*

Whether they planned it or not, those who toppled Sihanouk and who subsequently agreed to a confrontation between Cambodian forces and the Vietnamese Communists brought into being a situation in which their country was divided in a manner similar to the divisions which have existed in Laos since the early 1960's. This is the international significance of the March 1970 *coup d'état*. But the fundamental motivations of those who acted against Sihanouk stemmed from internal causes and reflected the continuing importance of elite rivalry as a major factor in the instability of countries in the Southeast Asian region.

* Son Ngoc Thanh's close involvement in the planning of the *coup d'état* was revealed to the author in the course of a visit to Saigon in January 1971 when he was able to interview Thanh's brother, Son Thai Nguyen.

# Chapter 10

# Theorists and Theories

No Southeast Asian Mao Tse-tung has provided a significant body of original thought, or even a major refinement of earlier writings on guerrilla tactics, which may be taken as a blueprint for revolt in the region. General Vo Nguyen Giap, as perhaps the most notable of the military leaders of 'a people's war' in Southeast Asia, has built on many of Mao's ideas, but the dominant impression of his writings is of subjective reactions to particular situations rather than a general theory which would apply to other countries than Viet-Nam. General Nasution's account of guerrilla warfare in Indonesia reads more like a *post hoc* justification for the events of the Indonesian Revolution than a handbook which provides a key to the implementation of tactics and strategy elsewhere.

Such reserved estimates of the strategic contributions contained in the writings of Giap and Nasution, or of non-military theoreticians on revolt and revolution such as North Viet-Nam's Truong Chinh, should not be taken as a denigration of these men's capacities as revolutionary leaders. General Nasution was an able military commander in the battles fought against the Dutch. Truong Chinh and General Giap showed a remarkable capacity to apply the lessons of other revolutionary situations in the course of the long battle against the French, and, although there is still no definite end in sight for the Second Indochinese War, their impact on the development of that conflict has been profound.

But if it is necessary to qualify the all-too-easily accorded eulogies which surround the names of successful guerrilla leaders in Southeast Asia, there is no less need for qualification of the abilities and perspicacity which has so often been seen as reflected in the writings of Western commentators on Asian revolt. Frequently possessing a background of military training, many of these commentators gird their opinions about with the most impervious ideological armour. For the historian who recognizes the impossibility of writing 'objective history' but trains himself to detect bias in others', if not always in his own, writing, the persistent impression provided by the contributions of the Western theorists is of an inability to accept that their view of the world may not be held by others to have an absolute validity. Beginning their analyses with a lack of sympathy for other than measured change through the actions of 'established governments', their hopes become their expectations to an extraordinary degree.

No one can approach a discussion of the various theories advanced to encourage or counter guerrilla warfare in Southeast Asia without confronting the philosophic problems involved in considering the use of violence in a political context. At the simplest level the United States Government's arguments concerning 'aggression from the North' in South Viet-Nam are a statement that no group should be permitted to achieve its political aims through military means. The extent to which the United States has itself on occasion fallen short of this ideal does not require emphasis.

The view from the other side puts the problem in perspective. The most notable Asian theoretician of the twentieth century has made famous his view that 'a revolution is not a dinner party'. When Mao Tse-tung made this point he was indicating not merely his awareness of the intellectual doubts of various of his colleagues as to the course which the Chinese Revolution was to follow. In his comment he affirmed the *revolutionary* nature of his political position, and his acceptance that revolutionary goals may have to be pursued through military means. It is the commitment to revolution which is so important in Mao's writings, and in Giap's. Mao Tse-tung's military thought built solidly upon that of the ancient Chinese strategist Sun Tzu, just as Vo Nguyen Giap's military ideas show a general acceptance of Mao's most important basic principles – the concept of liberation wars fought in three phases; the need to involve the peasants in the overall nature of a battle against the enemy; the careful balance which has to be achieved between political and military goals. An able strategist with totally different political commitments could have recognized the values of these concepts. What has been so hard for Western analysts to accept has been the importance of an ideological commitment in combination with military skills, and the fact that in some situations their own penchant for gradual and constitutional change may have little relevance for the people of the country in which a revolt or revolution takes place.

There is no need to subscribe to historical theories of inevitability to explain why Communist revolutions succeeded in China and Viet-Nam, but did not in either Malaya or the Philippines. In both the cases where Communist-led revolutions triumphed the high quality of leadership and the extraordinary relevance which Marxist theory had to the conditions which prevailed, in the eyes of the leaders and their followers, played a vital part in bringing success. It was not merely that conditions were 'ripe' for change, since there is abundant evidence to suggest that misery need not bring successful revolt. Much more to the point was the fact that men led revolts with a belief in the need for a revolutionary transformation of society. It was the aims of that revolutionary transformation which led to condemnation of the process rather than the means which were used to achieve it. Western commentators who condemn the Chinese and Vietnamese Communist revolutions find no difficulty in lauding revolutions of the past which were themselves steeped in violence. There is excessive simplification, but truth nonetheless, in the suggestion that if Chiang Kai-shek had fought on to victory, or if Ngo Dinh Diem had been able to ferment a successful revolt in North Viet-Nam then this would have been acceptable and, even more, highly commendable in the eyes of many Western analysts. In short, the yardstick for judgement in the eyes of so many commentators has little to do with violence, despite the emphasis which is placed on this aspect of a revolt or revolution, and is in fact basically dependent upon a decision as to the desirability of a particular political system which emerges at the end of the armed struggle.

There is a curious further aspect of this issue of judgement. While it is the nature of the system for which the revolutionary fights, rather than the way he fights, which determines the attitudes of so many commentators on insurgencies, the very unattractiveness of the system in the commentator's eyes leads him to deny that it plays any significant part in spurring men to fight. The organizational skills of trained Communist cadres, and not the particular appeals which they make, nor the ideals which they extol, are seen as leading to the dedication of the enemy. Organization becomes the explanation. In fact, this emphasis on organization is a rationale which enables the critical commentator to avoid the paradox of his own position.

In drawing attention to the way in which value judgements of a sometimes less than obvious sort are involved in so much of the writing which has recently appeared on insurgencies in Southeast Asia, neither this present chapter nor this book is arguing against the right or even the desirability of a commentator adopting a moral position on contemporary affairs. What is capital, however, is a declaration of one's position. It is nothing new that the soldiers who fight on either side should believe that their cause is just. This has been the belief which has sustained fighting men from ancient times. But there is something more involved. The conviction that rightness lies only on one side runs the very real risk of preventing a commentator on revolt and revolution from understanding, let alone accepting, that revolt or revolution. Lack of sympathy, in the sense of failing to perceive the motivations of others, can so distort an attempt to assess a problem that the analyst is brought up short of the subtleties which underlie any major development. No other explanation seems satisfactorily to account for the blind failure of so many highly qualified observers to perceive the trend of events in Viet-Nam over the past fourteen years. The opposite case is not more defensible. A Marxist need not be the best analyst of a Marxist-oriented revolution.

The extent to which personal political beliefs distort and hinder judgement is one side of the picture. The other side, when one considers the limitations of so much Western commentary on Asian revolution, involves the consistent use of false analogy. In the most general sense the Chinese experience has been taken as applicable to other countries in the Asian region. Whether or not China is devoted to fomenting revolution throughout Asia – a dubious proposition at the best of times – a serious review of the nature of the Chinese Revolution and of the factors involved in its success brings the realization that this was an essentially particular event. The Chinese Revolution succeeded through the existence of a complex matrix of interacting factors. Failure to rally peasant support would have negated the organizational assistance provided through Communist identification. The venality of the Kuomintang was as important a cause for the Communists' success as was the austere probity which the Chinese Army demonstrated in its relations with the peasants. What is more, far too little attention is paid to those prescriptions which Mao provides on the nature of revolutionary war, which were not present in the other major Communist-led success in the period after the Second World War. The Viet-Minh fought against the French in a colonial, not a semi-colonial country, in contrast to China. And the size of the country did not accord with Mao's insistence on the need for vast spaces to permit judicious retreat.

Despite the importance which the events of the Chinese

Revolution have been accorded in the eyes of both the Southeast Asian revolutionaries and those who have set out to counter them, the experience of counter-insurgency operations in Malaya and the Philippines seems to have dominated much of the thinking of theorists concerned with Viet-Nam. The reason for this situation is easy enough to find. In the Philippines and in Malaya the Communist-led insurgencies were defeated. Yet the closer the attention paid to developments in the Huk rebellion and the Malayan Emergency, the more clear it becomes that the conditions which permitted the defeat of the insurgents were no less particular than those which permitted the success of the Chinese Communist revolutionaries.

The literature which has grown out of the Malayan and Philippines experience has stressed the need to battle for the 'hearts and minds' of the uncommitted population in any situation of revolt. In bald terms such a prescription is beyond dispute. But reiteration of the catch-phrase neither leads to a serious attempt to answer whether 'hearts and minds' were indeed 'won' in Malaya or the Philippines, nor comes to grips with the highly controversial issue of how one should battle for the allegiance of the population. There are military prescriptions, it is true. British advisers with Malayan experience have repeatedly expressed views in relation to Viet-Nam which stress the contrast between the slow, methodical extension of security during the Malayan Emergency and the American inclination to pursue their war aims in Viet-Nam through the use of massive firepower and the commitment of large-scale forces to combat. Those American advisers who participated in the operations against the Huk insurgents in the Philippines during the late forties and early fifties have placed considerable emphasis on the role played by a well-led Filipino Army and police force. Yet while the problem of providing a majority of the population with satisfactory levels of security through combined political and military operations is beyond argument, the issue of political allegiance clearly involves more complicated considerations.

Reverting to the Malayan and Philippines examples, how correct is it to suggest that General Templer and President Magsaysay were successful in their battle to gain an alternative allegiance on the part of the peasants from that which the insurgents sought to gain? As earlier chapters of this book have suggested, the issue may well be much more complicated than enthusiastic admirers of the operations carried out in the Philippines and Malaya have suggested. The outstandingly successful aspect of the Malayan Emergency was the interlocking of military and administrative endeavour in what was still a colonial situation. There was, additionally, measured progress towards political independence which permitted the government's forces in Malaya to ridicule the suggestion that only the Chinese guerrillas were fighting for the goal of an independent Malaya. Yet, with the success of the military and administrative effort, and with the eventual achievement of Malayan independence in 1957, is it really correct to argue that the Malayan Chinese who were the target of the 'hearts and minds' policy were won over to approval of the established political system?

To suggest that no political effect was achieved among the Chinese resident in Malaya would be rash. To suggest, however, that what was really achieved might be better considered as neutralization for a period appears more sensible. The events of May 1969 have made abundantly clear the extent to which considerable numbers of Chinese in Malaya, now Malaysia, feel no identification with the established system. If winning 'hearts' is a shorthand description of the need to establish some emotional attachment to the established order, this has still to be achieved. The winning of 'minds' seems even less likely when rational analysis of the Malaysian situation brings the constant awareness of the way in which the concepts underlying the established system involve a continuing acceptance of Malay political dominance. It would be unreasonable not to note that the situation in Malaysia, even after the ethnic clashes of 1969, is more attractive to a great number of its citizens than is the case for many other countries in Southeast Asia. This, however, is scarcely the point when one considers the theories on the suppression of revolt which have emerged from the Emergency experience. The issue which remains open to debate is whether or not the counter-insurgency efforts of that period had the political and psychological success which has so often been claimed for them.

Even the most sceptical of commentators have accepted the remarkable extent to which President Ramon Magsaysay was able to project the image of a government interested in the welfare of the peasants who formed the reservoir of recruits for the Huks of central Luzon. With the vitally important success of eliminating the Huk politburo behind him, Magsaysay's pledges of help to the peasantry played a major part in breaking the Huk hold over the impoverished farmers and agricultural workers for whom the appeal of the Huk programme lay in its promises of an end to absentee landlords and their rack rents. Superficially, then, the Philippines experience suggests that 'hearts and minds' were indeed won. More detailed analysis leaves a more qualified picture. The numbers who benefited from the civic aid programmes which formed much of Magsaysay's proclaimed policy were limited. The programmes themselves lost much of their impetus with Magsaysay's death. Even more importantly, the defeat of the Huks is best understood not in terms of the elimination of the peasants' grievances as in the extent to which Magsaysay and his American advisers were able to reinforce the existing, and strongly cohesive, social structure of the Philippines. With the long-established pattern of oligarchic dominance by the *ilustrados* and the Catholic Church, the inequities of Philippines society represent some of the strongest arguments for the proposition that peasant misery need not lead to political and social revolution. If during Magsaysay's tenure of the posts of Secretary of Defence and President he succeeded in persuading some dissidents of the continuing value of identification with the existing society, he neither assured an end to their grievances in the future nor won his battle against the Huks primarily in these terms.

The ultimate success of any government will lie in the extent to which it is able to maintain an identification between its leadership and its citizens. Many governments have remained in power over long periods without achieving this conjunction of interest, but continuing disjunction is an invitation to unrest. To this extent the emphasis which commentators have placed on the need for containing and suppressing insurgent movements through gaining the allegiance of the people is sensible. When one comes to review the tragedy of misplaced hopes and misunderstood developments in Viet-Nam, however, the aim of gaining the 'hearts and minds' assumes a different character. On the one hand the assumption was made that inducement to identify with the successive post-1954 governments in Saigon was, in many cases, more important than the provision of security. On the other hand the assumption was somehow made that the events which had preceded 1954 had left no permanent mark upon the people of Viet-Nam. The extent to which the Viet-Minh had controlled large numbers of the population of southern Viet-Nam was conveniently forgotten.

The distorting lens of false analogy was involved in both these mistakes. In the first case, indeed, more than false analogy played its part. There was in addition poor understanding. In the successive pacification schemes which have been introduced in South Viet-Nam there has often seemed little appreciation of the extent to which the vital resettlement programmes which played such a part in the control of the Malayan insurgent challenge brought a genuine guarantee of security to those who were resettled. In wiping clean the slate of Viet-Nam's history before 1954, the analysts prepared a fresh field for their plans which could then be developed on assumptions which attached all legitimacy in South Viet-Nam to the regime directed by Ngo Dinh Diem. As with the British colonial government in Malaya before 1957 and as with the Philippines Government during the Huk insurgency, the government of South Viet-Nam became an 'established government'. The concept of established governments is in many ways central to the thinking of those Western commentators on revolt in Southeast Asia in general, and in South Viet-Nam in particular.

At first glance, and for those who are not committed to revolutionary change, the need to support established governments against armed challenge seems almost a self-evident proposition. The prospect of holding a different attitude conjures up visions of anarchy for most observers. Yet one is entitled to ask whether unswerving attachment to a principle of support for established governments is not in need of considerable qualification in the case of much of the Third World, and not merely Southeast Asia. At the first level of analysis the principle appears to stem from externally determined judgements as to the possible consequences of sudden change upon the network of reciprocal political and economic relationships which exist between two or more countries. America's decision to intervene in Viet-Nam reflected a belief in the damaging political consequences of the spread of Communism in Southeast Asia, which was seen as likely to prevent the 'free' development of the existing non-Communist states. Sudden political change in Malaysia would, in the eyes of Australian observers for instance, pose a threat to an important source of rubber and disturb a political relationship which, if not without incident, has been marked by general good feeling.

Too often, however, the concern which has been expressed about the consequences of revolutionary change for the orderly development of newly independent or developing states has disguised a much more basic opposition on the part of a particular commentator to the prospect that revolutionary change might mean the institution of a Communist regime. There is irony in this situation. Western observers whose own states provide them with a reasonable degree of governmental probity and economic satisfaction find remarkably little difficulty in arguing that the underprivileged and disadvantaged of Asia should work to obtain their goals through those orderly processes which have only been a part of the European world for an historically brief period. There is further irony in the apparent assumption of so many commentators that only Communism is likely to mount a campaign for the introduction of the sort of revolutionary change which is likely to remove the existing non-modern aspects of life from the Asian scene. Few commentators are so unsubtle as to suggest that there is no alternative lying between the maintenance of regimes of one or other degree of authoritarianism and Communism. Yet the suspicion remains that for many Western observers of the Southeast Asian scene the likelihood of change and of social and economic reform under existing governments is far from strong.

Some of the factors underlying the ironic assumption that feared revolution coming from the left will provide the most likely path to change may be given ready summary. Not least important is the extent to which it is possible to argue that few of the existing Southeast Asian governments have a clear perception of the multiple problems which their states confront. Where there is a suggestion that some understanding of these problems exists doubt remains as to the readiness and willingness of the state's leaders to undertake the root and branch form of surgery which would provide the assurance of substantial change. The over-inflated bubble of assured Cambodian internal security puffed up for all the world to see by Prince Norodom Sihanouk has been pricked. There is ample evidence of regional disunity springing from a variety of causes throughout the country. Cambodia, too, has social problems, not least those posed by its underemployed and over-educated youth and the slow but significant perception in some sections of society of the profound gap between wealth and the absence of wealth which characterizes the lot of the urban elite and the poorer peasantry.

Thailand's insurgency problems may well be readily contained by its military-dominated government. Nonetheless, the evidence which has been available of Thai methods of controlling insurgent outbreaks, particularly among the tribal groups in the north of the country, has not suggested any deep understanding on the part of the government of the difficulties which attend any effort to bring within close supervision a section of the population which has previously lived largely outside the state's control.

The catalogue could continue with reference to Burma's apparent inability to achieve even the minimal consensus which other Southeast Asian states have achieved. Account must be taken of the Philippines and its chronic social and economic problems; of the deep disunity which seems likely to mark the development of the fictive state of Laos for decades, short of an unlikely, if logical, division of its territory between its traditional suzerains, Thailand and Viet-Nam; of Indonesia, where, whatever the governmental stability which has been achieved following the downfall of Sukarno, the magnitude of the social and economic demands made upon the state by the ever-growing population staggers the imagination of the external and internal observer alike; and of Malaya, where the final consequences of a continuing policy of Malay political dominance seem seldom considered by those who have control over that state's destinies.

A clear further reason for the view which sees only in Communism or another political philosophy of the left an approach leading to truly revolutionary change is the matter of leadership. Leadership on the right, basically concerned with the preservation of privilege, has never been hard to find in Southeast Asia. However they proclaim their aims, it is fair to portray all of the existing Southeast Asian regimes (with the notable exception of

North Viet-Nam) as governments dominated by men concerned with the preservation of existing elites. Burma's proclaimed dedication to socialism scarcely seems to qualify this comment.

Leadership genuinely concerned with the needs of the people has been a scarcer commodity. Even at the most cynical and critical assessment, leadership which *claims* to be concerned with the interests of the population at large has been in short supply. The fear that Communism might make further advances in Southeast Asia is usually couched in terms of the readiness among adherents of this revolutionary ideology to resort to violence. Once again this concern for political and economic change pursued through violence appears to distort an underlying preoccupation with the possibility that leadership of the sort which the Communists provide has a very real chance of effecting fundamental change. Reduced to the bluntest terms, adherence to Communism has not only led to the development of organizational skills, it has brought the emergence of men whose dedication to the success of their political programmes has been of a remarkable sort. That this dedication has not always led to success must be recognized as being the result of the inapplicability of these leaders' ideological answers to particular situations and the extent to which the social configuration of many Southeast Asian states still leaves the control of armed power firmly in the hands of conservative interests. The Marxist will be wrong in assuming that the advance of Communism is inevitable in Southeast Asia. But the entrenched leaders of Southeast Asian states would be equally wrong in assuming that they face no significant challenge in the future.

Challenge, it must be recognized, does not come merely because of the existence of social inequities and political discrimination. Challenge to existing systems emerges when through leadership and the provision of an alternative ideology a substantial proportion of the population comes to perceive the inequities of their position and the disadvantages under which they live their lives. The profound question which hangs over Southeast Asia is whether the changes which most Western commentators see as necessary can come as the result of the efforts of anyone other than those committed to revolutionary ideals. If this is not the case, will support of conservative entrenched governments be the only possibility open to the West?

The emphasis placed on the conceptual undergrowth which lies beneath the more prominently visible features of insurgency and counter-insurgency theory should not disguise the existence of a substantial body of increasingly sophisticated discussion of the problems associated with revolt and revolution. We do know more of the techniques which seem likely to produce success and failure for both the insurgent and those who seek to counter his efforts. The range of success which can be achieved through re-settlement programmes and the role played by military force, as opposed to political persuasion, are better understood now than in the early years of the Viet-Nam War. One can only presume that on the other side of the political and military fence study of the implications of various successes and failures has been no less careful.

This growing body of technical knowledge must, in the final analysis, be considered within the wider framework of the societies to which it is applied. External prescriptions may take account of an infinite number of variables in their attempts to prevent or suppress revolts. Yet no external force can replace the dedication which must be found internally if those prescriptions are to be carried through to fruition. The converse is equally important. The fantasy of revolts and revolutions conjured up from afar by hostile external forces has just as little reality. Revolts and revolutions are internal affairs and descriptions of them which involve such terms as 'aggression by proxy' are intellectually shabby and emotionally suspect. For the future, whether revolts succeed or fail will not be determined in Peking or Washington or Moscow. The material support which may come from these centres will be important, as will the ideologies which are espoused in them. But the ultimate determinants will be found in the countries of Southeast Asia; in the policies which are formulated by Southeast Asians; and in the extent to which Southeast Asian leaders are able to show that their concern is for change which is genuinely related to the aspirations and interests of the mass of the population which currently have so little sense of identification with the governments that rule over them.

# Chapter 11

# Region of Revolt

Western perceptions of the nature of Southeast Asian societies have changed radically since the Second World War. In part this reflects the slow disillusionment which accompanied the unsuccessful fight by the French and Dutch colonial governments to maintain their positions in the Indochinese region and in Indonesia. In part the change has stemmed from the realization that assumptions concerning the possibility of transforming Southeast Asian states into some copy, or at least approximation, of nations in the West were illusory. In some measure, probably a much smaller measure than Western scholars of Southeast Asia would wish to be the case, the change in perception reflects the growing body of knowledge on the part of those in the West about the more profound differences separating the societies of their own countries and those of the countries in the Southeast Asian region. The Western world's conscious image of the colonized states of Southeast Asia not only was distorted by the capacity which colonial governments appeared to have to 'freeze' the societies over which they ruled, so that many of the problems which lay beneath the surface were held in check until independence was achieved. At the same time it was easy, while colonial rule existed, for the impression to develop that the colonized peoples were both anxious, and in some cases even ready, to transform themselves into rather differently coloured Frenchmen, Dutchmen or Englishmen, devoted to the same concepts of parliamentary democracy which were held by their rulers.

The error of holding such assumptions is now abundantly clear. The inapplicability of Western-style democracy, in the eyes of the Southeast Asians themselves, has been demonstrated time and again. Military regimes are in control in Burma, Thailand, Indonesia and South Viet-Nam. Authoritarian regimes of one variety or another control the destinies of Cambodia, North Viet-Nam and, for the moment, Malaya. The future of democracy in the Philippines may be less uncertain than many observers have been led to believe following the 1969 elections, but there is certainly reason to argue that the parliamentary and presidential systems as these exist in that country are less than in accord with the high ideals of democratic government to which Western nations subscribe, even if these ideals are not always practised.

It may be that the slow rundown of Western participation in the Vietnamese War will signal the end of excessively optimistic expectations for the future development of Southeast Asia. Whatever the ultimate outcome of the conflict in Viet-Nam the strong indications at the beginning of the seventies are that the United States will never again become involved in a war of this magnitude in Southeast Asia and that in the future Southeast Asian states will be expected to meet their own internal challenges rather than to hope that their battles will be fought for them. This is not to argue that an eventual United States withdrawal from Viet-Nam will be the signal for cataclysmic change in the Southeast Asian region. Nor is it even to argue that the lack of a major Western presence in the region is likely to spur on the efforts of those who wish to achieve change through revolutionary means. If revolts continue to be a significant feature in the modern history of Southeast Asian states this will be a reflection of the multitude of unsolved social, political and economic problems which abound in those states and which still remain to be solved, or in some cases even to be recognized. For Southeast Asian governments it is probably correct to suggest that there has been a similar scaling down of the hopeful expectations which they, in similar fashion to Western observers, held for the future. The great imponderable is the degree to which a diminution of hopeful expectations has also been accompanied by a readiness to work for the changes necessary to forestall revolt and revolution.

Without embarking upon a detailed review of developments in all the states of Southeast Asia a case may certainly be made to show that the past few years have seen the qualification of many earlier assumptions and the appearance of many new problems, or of old problems in a new and more complex guise. The sudden transformation of the situation in Cambodia as the result of a revolt from the right provides a clear example of the way in which old assumptions can be both rapidly and radically revised.

It is clear that the decision taken by members of the Cambodian conservative elite to overthrow Prince Norodom Sihanouk was the result, in part, of their concern for the extent to which Cambodian territory in the eastern regions of the country had come under the control of Vietnamese Communist forces. Yet this 'external' fact is probably most correctly viewed as being the catalyst which set in motion a reaction based, essentially, on internal considerations.

The image of Cambodia which Prince Sihanouk and his government presented to the world since the achievement of independence in 1953 was that of a much beloved leader of royal descent dealing energetically with the task of transforming his country into a modern state. But the Cambodian leader's energy and goodwill were insufficient to overcome some of the major problems which beset the country. Sihanouk was not the only Third World leader who was unable to devise a satisfactory set of political institutions which could provide both an opportunity to resolve political rivalries within the state and for the functioning of political bodies in association with them. The creation in 1955 of the mass political movement, the Sangkum Reastr Niyum (People's Socialist Community), was a master-stroke at a time when an end to party squabbling was earnestly desired by the major interest groups within the country. It proved to be a less satisfactory answer by the end of the sixties, with the realization among Cambodians along the range of the political spectrum that one man's personal rule gave little guarantee that their interests would be served.

The deteriorating situation in Cambodia in the closing years of the sixties went unrecognized by a great many commentators because of the emotional and political appeal which Prince Sihanouk's policies had for observers disenchanted with the authoritarian regimes of the right and the left which govern so many Southeast Asian states. Prince Sihanouk's dazzling personality and his apparent success in both the international and domestic spheres obscured the extent to which the Phnom Penh elite – his most important supporters – were growing more and more disillusioned with their leader's policies.

In mounting their *coup d'état* the new leaders in Cambodia opened a Pandora's box of staggeringly large dimensions with consequences so considerable that it is probably appropriate to speak of Sihanouk's deposition as marking the end of an era. In a more general sense, however, the point to grasp is that the governance of Cambodia in the closing years of the sixties became much more difficult, in terms of both perceptions and actual problems, than was the case at the beginning of the decade. Old, optimistic assumptions which seemed so reassuring in the period shortly after independence have now disappeared and instead the difficulties stemming from unsolved problems are in clear view.

A similar slow erosion of the optimistic expectations which accompanied independence may be ascribed to Malaysia, and more particularly to Malaya, the dominant partner in the Federation. Malaya's accession to independence in 1957 appeared as a triumph of reason and tolerance over the twin challenges of Communist subversion and the dangers of ethnic rivalry. The passage of more than ten years has provided a perspective with which to make rather more critical judgements concerning the assumptions involved in the achievement of Malayan

187

independence. And the experience of some twelve years of independence provides the evidence of the continuing unsolved problems which confront Malaysia.

This was shown dramatically in the events of May 1969 when the passions which had been obscured beneath the surface of apparent racial tolerance, if not complete racial harmony, broke through in the form of tragic confrontations between Malays and Chinese. The detailed causes of the 13 May incident in Kuala Lumpur still cannot be stated with any accuracy. The Malaysian Government's disposition to treat the affair in terms of a Communist-inspired outbreak involving discontented Malayan Chinese scarcely bears any critical examination. What does seem apparent is that, after years in which informed observers of Malayan and Malaysian politics have foreseen the likelihood of a breakdown occurring in Malaya because of the disadvantages endured by the Chinese segment of the population, the ethnic clashes which did occur owed as much to the resentment of poorer Malays at what they felt was their inability to share in the economic advantages of the state.

Stated baldly, but nonetheless accurately, the political formula which was introduced at the time Malaya became independent assumed that for an indefinite period Malays would hold a firm grip on political power while Chinese would be content with the considerable commercial prospects available within the country. It would be optimistic, at the beginning of the seventies, to suggest that this formula is still an answer to Malaysia's problems. There is little indication that Malays are ready to make an adjustment to their place within the arrangement. Indeed, since May 1969 a strong case might be made to suggest that there are significant indications of a hardening of Malay political opinion in terms of even firmer control of all matters of importance by Malays as opposed to citizens of other races. Any thought which was present in 1956 that the Alliance formula might eventually lead to the development of non-communal political parties in Malaya has now effectively disappeared.

But due attention should also be paid to the less dramatic, yet no less significant, aspects of the Malaysian scene which are symptomatic of the now outdated character of the political agreements devised at the time of independence. Malaysia, in company with the other countries of Southeast Asia which emerged from colonial rule after the Second World War, has placed a high premium on education. The difficulty involved in such a policy is the high level of success achieved by Chinese students at all levels of the educational system and the relatively limited number of places which are open to these students, both at universities and within the civil service. The problem is not yet acute but it is clearly present. The reservation of a specific proportion of places for Malays in both the universities and the public service may have seemed justified in the middle fifties when it was still possible to believe that some time limit might be set on the position. The difficulty is to convince able Chinese candidates for places that independent Malaysia must continue to discriminate against talent along ethnic lines.

It is easy to be excessively gloomy about Malaysia just because of the magnitude of the problems which the leaders of that country must confront. It may be that the very size of the problems will act as a caution to those persons whose inclinations in the future are to seek a quick rather than a gradual solution to the difficulties posed by ethnic and political imbalance. The continuing hopeful prospects for Malaysia's economy, despite the inherent dangers associated with a limited range of export commodities, are a further likely buffer to the sudden collapse of the existing governing elite. Whatever may be the case for Malaysia's future prospects, however, the fact remains that much of the optimism which existed in the immediate *Merdeka* period has now evaporated. The possibility of ethnic disagreement becoming ethnic violence is now clearly apparent. One may still ask, however, whether ethnic division is now no longer seen merely as an out-growth of Communism.

The experience of both Cambodia and Malaysia should alert us to the way in which a series of quite fundamental problems may now be perceived which, for a variety of reasons, have been submerged or ignored over the past decade, and particularly over the past few years in which analysis of the region has been so heavily concerned with the international politics of Southeast Asia. This estimation is not made in terms of Western interests, however loosely such interests may be defined, but in terms of the Southeast Asian countries' need to readjust their own assumptions and preconceptions. If one seeks for a blanket description of this state of affairs the words of a Southeast Asian politician offer one general characterization of the situation. The Singapore Minister for Foreign Affairs, Mr S. Rajaratnam, has been quoted as referring to the 1950s as an 'age of confidence' and to the 1960s as an 'age of disillusionment'.

The danger with this terminology, as with all general estimations, is that it may disguise the subtleties and the variants which are present. At the general level, however, the contrast between optimism and disillusionment is a useful analytical tool. Viewed in these terms, it was not only Cambodia and Malaysia which, some ten or twelve years ago, faced the future reasonably secure in their assumptions that it was manageable and that no major problems existed within the state which could not be solved as a result of the mobilization of national will. The dangers of tribal dissidence and regional discontent were scarcely noted in Thailand during the late 1950s. Following the collapse of the regional rebellions in Indonesia the path along which President Sukarno was to lead his country was not seen as strewn with difficulties of political conflict by the majority of the politically conscious, no matter what judgements are now made with the wisdom of hindsight. For Burma and Laos, continually plagued by the deep ethnic divisions which are such a hindrance

to any real national unity, the end of the fifties may not
have held the same prospect of a settled future. Nevertheless, it is possible to detect some assumption by the Burmese military officers who seized power in 1962 that their
intervention would bring a solution to Burma's perennial
ills, just as their predecessors had believed in 1948 when
Burma became independent. And even Laotian politicians, who had such small reason for optimism in the face
of their almost insuperable problems, appear to have believed that the 1962 Laotian settlement, while not a final
solution, would open the way to a less troubled period.
In the Philippines the final years of the fifties seemed more
assured than those at the end of the sixties. The successful containment of the Huk challenge and the apparent
concern of the Philippines Government with social issues
provided promising auguries for the future, as also did
the possibility of the emergence of a significant group of
Filipino entrepreneurs.

To the extent that one can generalize from them, the
experiences of Cambodia and Malaysia suggest that the
leadership which emerged at the time of independence
was less than satisfactorily equipped to understand or
to perceive the problems of a post-independence situation. Colonial rule froze or rendered latent many of the
most significant problems within the state and those who
worked for independence did not have to contend with
these problems until after the colonial ruler had departed.
There seem, in fact, to be two broad divisions into which
post-independence problems might be divided. The first
are those which are inherent to or traditionally part of any
state, the second those which emerge as a result of inex-
pertly conceived policies on the part of the independent
leaders. Indonesia's traditional problems involving ethnic
and regional rivalry were submerged for a period by the
experience of the Indonesian Revolution. There was for a
time an assessment that 'Unity in Diversity' could be not
only an ideal but also a fact. The experience of the regional rebellions provided the qualification. It was not

until the middle sixties, however, that the dangers and problems associated with President Sukarno's domination of politics were finally perceived by a large enough group of politically conscious men who also could agree on the need for action.

The one country which did not experience colonial rule does not escape the assessment that Southeast Asian leaders during the fifties failed to grasp many of the essential internal problems facing their countries. Singularly fortunate as the result of its ethnic homogeneity, Thailand nevertheless must find some solution to the problems of relations with its tribal minorities. Left alone, as was the traditional practice, the hill tribes posed little difficulty to the majority government. This was the case so long as the tribal groups did not have any sense of their disadvantages. The necessity, for the Thai Government, of expanding contact with the tribal groups, in the face of the threat of subversion, has illustrated only too clearly that the tribal groups are disadvantaged and made the work of subversion easier. In the northeast of Thailand the growth of serious problems for the Thai Government as the result of a widespread feeling that to be a northeasterner is to be disadvantaged reflects the difficulty which Bangkok-centred politicians have had in perceiving the interests of their more distant compatriots.

Throughout the states of Southeast Asia one may perceive the problems which arise because of the rivalries which exist between ethnic groups. In both Malaysia and Indonesia the position of the overseas Chinese is difficult. In other countries of the region the rivalry is between the dominant lowland groups and the traditionally disadvantaged uplands people who are so frequently regarded as 'barbarians'. Consideration of southern Viet-Nam has been excluded from this chapter because of the great uncertainty which attaches to its future. Yet in that region, perhaps as dramatically as anywhere else in the Southeast Asian area, the rivalry between the Vietnamese and the tribal *moi* is bitter and deep-seated. The problems which follow upon the increasing availability of education are equally widespread in the region. This particular problem has become apparent in recent years. It is still far from clear that any of the governments which must deal with it fully understand the implications of their continued stress on the desirability of increasing educational opportunities with far too little concern for the quality and nature of that education.

But not all of the new perceptions which suggest a significant level of change throughout Southeast Asia should be viewed in pessimistic terms. That the future carries with it the very real threat of unrest, revolt and even revolution in the countries of Southeast Asia should scarcely be surprising once one comes to recognize the long distance which so many of them still have to travel along the path towards modernization and true attainment of nation status. Acting against this perception has been the continuing readiness of Western governments to believe that through their intervention major adjustments could be made to what were, essentially, the internal problems of Southeast Asian states. The experience of Viet-Nam has, presumably, changed this estimation.

Yet even here, Viet-Nam is amongst the last rather than the first of the coffin nails in the Western assumptions about Southeast Asian politics. The fact of United States hesitation over future involvement in Thailand is not merely a reflection of the American experience in Viet-Nam. It is a reaction which follows upon a series of developments in which Western efforts to change the course of Southeast Asian history have been less than successful. The combined force of American aid and political influence in Indonesia did not sway Sukarno's policies and change came after the United States had reduced its interests in that country. The Laotian settlement was conceived by its non-Asian sponsors, both Communist and non-Communist, as a solution to the dangers of international rivalry in an obscure region. The rivalry was reduced, but no real solution to Laos' perennial problems was found. British efforts to tidy up a colonial heritage in the Malaysian region through the association of a number of disparate states at first appeared desirable to both Malayans and Singaporeans, but the Malaysia plan which had such strong British backing brought the forced secession of Singapore when the dominant Southeast Asians in the Federation felt that the plan was no longer workable. American assumptions about the relationship between the United States and the Philippines have gone through continual qualification as Filipino politicians have found that nationalism does not sit happily with client status.

Concentration on the internal factors at work within the various Southeast Asian states is in no sense an argument against the undoubted fact that external involvement can affect the destinies of individual countries. The fantasies of China's close direction of the Viet-Nam War have passed, but there is no way in which Southeast Asian states whose borders are contiguous with China's can ignore the size and interests of their massive neighbour. So long as America chooses to maintain a presence in Southeast Asia this will be a factor in the course which the region as a whole follows. In a less formidable, but no less important fashion the opportunities for interference in the affairs of one country by another in the region will long remain.

Southeast Asia in the seventies can scarcely avoid its measure of difficulties and troubles as the result of the mass of unsolved problems which confront even the most successful of the governments in the region. It seems proper to suggest that all the evidence which is currently available points towards an absence of cataclysms, but it leaves the strong possibility of recurring revolt. The long history of revolt in the region is insufficient basis for an expectation that instances of revolt will mark the future as they have marked the past. The continued existence of so many of the factors which have led to past revolt is, however, a strong reason for believing that many years have still to pass before true stability can replace the transient calm which seems the best hope for the region in the near future.

# Bibliography

There is a vast body of writing concerned with the issue of revolt and revolution in Southeast Asia. Much of this writing is, however, of an essentially technical character and the works listed in this Bibliography are selected for their general interest and for their relevance to questions raised in the text of the book. Many of the books listed provide detailed bibliographies of their own.

Benda, H. J., 'Peasant Movements in Colonial Southeast Asia', *Asian Studies* III, 3 (December 1965), 420-34.
———— 'The Communist Rebellions of 1926-27 in Indonesia', *Pacific Historical Review* XXIV (1955), 139-52.
Brimmel, J. H., *Communism in Southeast Asia*, London 1959.
Buttinger, J., *Vietnam: A Dragon Embattled* (2 vols), New York 1967.
Clutterbuck, R. L., *The Long, Long War*, New York 1966.
Cross, J. E., *Conflict in the Shadows*, New York 1963.
Devillers, Ph., *Histoire du Viêt-Nam de 1942 à 1952*, Paris 1952.
Duncanson, D. J., *Government and Revolution in Vietnam*, London 1968.
Fairbairn, G., *Revolutionary Warfare and Communist Strategy*, London 1968.
Fall, B. B., *Street Without Joy*, Harrisburg, Pa., 1963.
———— *The Two Viet-Nams* (2nd rev. ed.), New York 1967.
Galula, D., *Counterinsurgency Warfare*, New York 1964.
Girling, J. L. S., *People's War*, London 1969.
Hall, D. G. E., *A History of Southeast Asia*, London 1964.
Ho Chi Minh, *Selected Works* (4 vols), Hanoi 1961.

Bibliography

Jacoby, E. H., *Agrarian Unrest in Southeast Asia* (2nd ed.), London 1961.

Kahin, G. McT., and Lewis, J. W., *The United States in Vietnam* (2nd ed.), New York 1969.

Kautsky, J. H., *Political Change in Underdeveloped Countries*, New York 1963.

Lancaster, D., *The Emancipation of French Indo-China*, London 1961.

Lieberman, V., 'Why the Hukbalahap movement failed', *Solidarity* I, 4 (October-December 1966), 23-30.

Mao Tse-tung, *Selected Works of Mao Tse-tung* (4 vols), Peking 1965.

Nasution, A. H., *Fundamentals of Guerrilla Warfare*, New York 1965.

O'Neill, R. J., *General Giap: Politician and Strategist*, Melbourne 1969.

Osborne, M. E., *Strategic Hamlets in South Viet-Nam: A Survey and a Comparison*, Cornell Southeast Asia Program Data Paper No. 55, Ithaca, N.Y., 1965.

———— *The French Presence in Cochinchina and Cambodia*, Ithaca, N.Y., 1969.

Paret, P., and Shy, J. W., *Guerrillas in the 1960's* (2nd ed.), New York 1962.

Pike, D., *Viet Cong*, Cambridge, Mass., 1966.

Pye, L., *Guerrilla Communism in Malaya*, Princeton, N.J., 1956.

Scaff, A., *The Philippine Answer to Communism*, Stanford, Cal., 1955.

Tanham, G. K., *Communist Revolutionary Warfare* (2nd ed.), New York 1967.

Thompson, R., *Defeating Communist Insurgency*, London 1966.

———— *No Exit from Vietnam*, London 1969.

Tilman, R., 'The Non-Lessons of the Malayan Emergency', *Asian Survey* VI, 8 (August 1966), 407-19.

Trager, F. (ed.), *Marxism in Southeast Asia*, Stanford, Cal., 1959.

Trinquier, R., *Modern Warfare*, New York 1964.

Bibliography

Truong Chinh, *The Resistance Will Win*, Hanoi 1960.
Valeriano, N. D., and Bohannan, C. T., *Counter Guerrilla Operations: The Philippine Experience*, New York 1962.
Van der Kroef, J. M., 'Prince Diponegoro: progenitor of Indonesian nationalism', *Far Eastern Quarterly* VIII, 4 (August 1949), 424-50.
Vo Nguyen Giap, *People's War, People's Army*, Hanoi 1961.
Warner, D., *The Last Confucian*, New York 1963.

# Index

Agroville Scheme, 143

Bao Dai, Emperor, 77, 78, 116-17
Briggs Plan, 92
British forces in Viet-Nam, 113
Burma, 25, 26, 27, 32, 36, 55, 80-81, 181, 190-91
Burmese Independence Army, 80

Cambodia, 22, 23, 24, 28, 31, 32, 45-51, 68-80, 179, 186-7, 190-91
Cambodian *coup d'etat* of 1970, 159-68 *passim*
Cambodian Rising of 1885-6, 11-12, 36, 37, 45-50
Categories of Revolt, 18
  revolts against foreign domination, 18, 21, 34-5
  revolts involving elite rivalry, 18, 23, 24
  revolts of regions and minorities, 19-20, 25
  millenarian revolts, 20, 31-2, 35
Chinese in Malaya (Malaysia), 69, 70, 83-4, 88-9, 91, 98, 175, 188
Chinese Nationalist forces in Viet-Nam, 113
Chinese People's Republic and Viet-Nam, 124
Chinese Revolution, 170, 172-3
Chinese squatters in Malaya, 89-90, 92, 93
Chin Peng, 97
Chou En-lai, 127
Colonial impact on Cambodia, 45, 68
  on Malaya, 70

on Southeast Asia, 15, 16, 34, 53, 71, 72, 184
on Viet-Nam, 41-2
Communism in Malaya (Malaysia), 88-92, 97-9, 189-90
the Philippines, 105
Southeast Asia, 171, 173-4, 179, 180, 181
Viet-Nam, 14, 53, 54, 58, 59, 60, 77, 111-12, 119-21, 128-9, 132, 152-3, 157, 158
Communist revolts in Indonesia of 1926-7, 12, 64-7
Counter-insurgency theory: *see* Insurgency and counter-insurgency theory

D'Argenlieu, Admiral, 113, 122
De Gaulle, General Charles, 113, 122
De Lattre de Tassigny, General, 122
Dien-Bien-Phu, 13, 123-6
Diponegoro, Prince, 37-40

Eisenhower, Dwight D., 134, 142

Fall, Bernard, 120, 126
First Indochinese War: *see* Franco-Viet-Minh War
Franco-Viet-Minh War, 111-29, 158
Franco-Viet-Minh War and opposition in France, 122

Geneva Conference on Indochina, 126, 131, 135

# Index

Gia Long, Emperor, 28

Ham Nghi, Emperor, 42-4
Hatta, M., 81
Ho Chi Minh, 14, 57-9, 75, 77, 78, 111-16, 119, 123, 128, 134, 137
Huks (Hukbalahap), 84-5, 101-10, 174, 176

Indonesia, 12, 23, 27-8, 37-41, 81-3, 180, 190, 191
Indonesian Communist revolts of 1926-7: see Communist revolts in Indonesia
Insurgency and counter-insurgency theory, 170-74, 182

Japanese occupation of Southeast Asia, 74, 75-6
Java War, 37-41
Johnson, Lyndon B., 149, 154

Lansdale, General, 101
Laos, 77-80 passim, 180, 190-91, 193-4
Leclerc, General, 113
Le Van Khoi revolt, 29-31
Lon Nol, General, 159, 165, 167

Magsaysay, President, 101, 106-10, 175, 176-7
Malaya (Malaysia), 36-7, 68-71, 83-4, 88-101, 175-6, 180, 187-90, 191, 194
Malayan Chinese Association, 95
Malayan Communist Party, 89
Malayan Emergency, 83-4, 90-101, 174-5, 176
Malays, 83, 188
Malaysian riots of 1969, 176, 188
Mao Tse-tung, 169, 170-71
Mendès-France, Pierre, 126
Molotov, Vyacheslav M., 127
Monique, Madame, 164, 165, 166
McNamara, Robert, 148

Nasution, General Abdul, 169
National Liberation Front for South Viet-Nam, 14, 140, 141, 154-6, 160-63, 167
Nationalism in Malaya, 83
Southeast Asia, 35, 50, 52-3, 54
Viet-Nam, 14, 41, 45, 54, 59, 77, 111-12, 121, 127-9, 132, 153, 158
Navarre, General, 124
Nghe-An Soviets, 12, 56, 60, 61
Ngo Dinh Diem, 116, 127, 131-42 passim, 147, 178
Ngo Dinh Nhu, 137, 140, 144
Norodom, King, 46-9
Norodom Sihanouk, King and Prince, 79, 159-68 passim, 179, 186-7

Pacification in Viet-Nam, 156
Pahang War, 36
Phan Boi Chau, 57
Philippines, 55, 84-5, 101-10, 180, 191
Pomeroy, William, 108

Quirino, President, 105

Resettlement Programme in Malaya, 93-7, 100

Sadkalist movement, 55
Saya San revolt, 36, 55
Scholars' revolt in Viet-Nam, 37, 41-5
Second Indochinese War: see Viet-Nam War
Second World War: impact on Burma, 80-81
impact on Cambodia, 77-80
impact on Indonesia, 81-3
impact on Laos, 77-8, 79-80
impact on Malaya and Singapore, 83-4
impact on Philippines, 84-5
impact on Southeast Asia, 72, 74, 75, 86-7

Second World War—*cont.*
  impact on Thailand, 85
  impact on Viet-Nam, 77-80
Sihanouk: *see* Norodom Siha-
  nouk
Singapore, 83-4
Sirik Matak, 159, 167
Son Ngoc Thanh, 79, 168
Souphanouvong, Prince, 79
Strategic Hamlet Program, 142-8
Strategic Hamlet Program and
  British experience in Ma-
  laya, 145-7
Sukarno, President, 81, 190, 192,
  193

Taruc, Luis, 103, 108
Templer, General Sir Gerald, 95,
  96, 175
Tet offensive of 1968, 154, 155,
  156
Thailand, 28, 55, 85, 180, 192
Thompson, Sir Robert, 144
Ton That Thuyet, 42, 44
Trung sisters, 11, 21

Truong Chinh, 149, 169

United States of America and the
  Viet-Nam War, 133, 135,
  141-2, 148, 149-53, 159, 168,
  178, 185, 193

Viet-Minh, 13, 77-80, 112-15,
  119-22, 124, 137-8, 177
Viet-Minh cadres, 137, 138, 140
Viet-Nam, 12, 13, 14, 21, 25, 26,
  28, 29, 30, 41-5, 57-63, 77-80,
  110, 111-29, 130-58, 192-3
Viet-Nam War, 130-58, 173-4,
  177, 185
  and Cambodia, 159-68 *passim*
Vietnamese Nationalist Party, 59,
  62
Vo Nguyen Giap, 77, 118-19, 149,
  155, 169, 170, 171

Westmoreland, General William,
  150
Wheeler, General Earle, 148

Yen-Bay mutiny, 60